Second Edition

Business Anthropology

Second Edition

Business Anthropology

Ann T. Jordan
University of North Texas

WAVELAND

PRESS, INC.

Long Grove, Illinois

For information about this book, contact:
  Waveland Press, Inc.
  4180 IL Route 83, Suite 101
  Long Grove, IL 60047-9580
  (847) 634-0081
  info@waveland.com
  www.waveland.com

Contents

Acknowledgments

Ten years after the publication of the first edition of this book, it is satisfying to see the publication of a second edition and to contemplate the ways in which the field of business anthropology has grown and developed internationally. I salute all my colleagues who work in this field both inside and outside academia and regret I was not able to discuss more of their work in this volume.

I wish to thank Tom Curtin and Jeni Ogilvie at Waveland Press for their friendship and their help with my publications over the last ten years. This has made publishing with Waveland a pleasure. I appreciate the continued support of the anthropology department at the University of North Texas and thank my family, Dennis, Mark, Peter, and Andrew, for their patience and love. Any errors in this book are, of course, my own.

Chapter One

The Anthropological Approach

Anthropology is known for its work in places that seem exotic to Westerners. Yet, anthropologists have long been involved analyzing human behavior in Western industrial and business settings. When I begin a new fieldwork project, there is much to be done. I check my cameras, tape recorders, tablet, and laptop computer to be sure they are all in working order. I stock up on batteries. I consider my clothing. I need clothing that is durable, befitting of the climate, and appropriate for the culture I will be studying. I make connections with the host communities. I work out necessary travel arrangements—make reservations for air and land transport, and determine where I will stay. I am ready to go.

I arrive by plane at my destination and set off early the next morning for my fieldwork site. Dressed in culturally appropriate clothing, a conservative business suit, with my briefcase in hand, I navigate the rush hour traffic, finally arriving at my fieldwork site, a structure of glass and metal on a busy downtown street. It is a high-rise office building in a large southwestern city in the United States. I am a business anthropologist; I apply my skills in complex organizations, and I am at this field site to work with a multinational corporation. I will conduct ethnographic fieldwork much as all anthropologists around the world do, but not with, for example, farmers in Rajasthan or the Sherpas near Mount Everest. I will be working with individuals in a US corporation.

In ethnographic fieldwork, I personally experience the lives of the individuals in their natural setting in order to write a description of their ways of life. This way of understanding relies mainly on qualitative research methods, and the description I write is called an ethnography. Many other social scientists primarily use quantitative methods; the

1

researcher gathers data that can be reduced to numbers and analyzed using statistics. An example of statistical data would be that 25 percent of the people residing in Saudi Arabia are immigrants to that country. Further quantitative data might give the percentage of immigrants in each of ten job categories. Qualitative data gathered on the same subject might include interviews with the immigrants about their experience living in Saudi Arabia. Here the researcher's analysis would be a descriptive explanation of how immigrants adapt to life in Saudi Arabia.

Frequently, researchers combine quantitative and qualitative data. The statistics provide a valuable summary and analysis of the subject, which the qualitative data enriches by providing an understanding of what the statistics mean in people's real lives. Not only do anthropologists make more use of qualitative methods than most other social scientists, they have a specific approach to understanding human behavior, particularly group behavior and culture. They look at the ways the customs and beliefs of a people are interrelated (holism), compare groups of people around the world and across cultures to get a larger understanding of human behavior (cross-cultural comparison), and try to understand behavior from the participant's point of view rather than their own personal one (cultural relativism).

In anthropology there are multiple theoretical approaches; all of them concern the reasons humans behave as they do. Some anthropologists favor scientific and evolutionary approaches that suggest cultural differences can be explained by differing human adaptations to differing natural and social environments. This kind of explanation is at the heart of *cultural ecology* and of *materialism*, two anthropological theoretical perspectives. In the *functionalist theoretical approach*, cultural features are explained by the way they function to make the culture work. If some feature, polygynous marriage for example, did not contribute to the persistence of the entire culture, then it would have disappeared. In the latter half of the twentieth century, *a postmodern approach* became important in anthropology. Advocates of this approach think human cultures are too complex to be explained by any general theory; to them, it is more valuable to understand behavior from the point of view of the group of humans who are being studied. More recently, *complexity theory* and the study of complex adaptive systems have become important approaches to understanding globalization.

In all cases, however, anthropological theories are concerned with that peculiar perspective of anthropology that combines holism, cross-cultural comparison, and relativism, although the value of these three is stressed differently by members of each theoretical school. For example, while all the theoretical approaches mentioned above would stress holism, postmodernists would make less use of cross-cultural comparison than materialists would. Business anthropologists make use of the entire array of anthropological theoretical approaches, including the ones above.

TACKLING IMPORTANT ISSUES

I call the subfield of anthropology that is the subject of this book "business anthropology," but as I construe it and as anthropologists practice it, business anthropology is not limited to for-profit companies. A business anthropologist works with for-profit organizations, such as General Motors or Intel, and nonprofit organizations, such as the Red Cross, as well as with government organizations at the local, state, and federal levels. The organizations vary in size from large corporations, such as Toyota, to small family-owned businesses, such as a local veterinary clinic. The subject of a "business" anthropologist's work is the behavior in and around any organization or the behavior of the consumers of products and services provided by an organization. Whether they are working for nonprofit or for-profit organizations, these anthropologists are studying many business issues including work process, group behavior, organizational change, diversity, and globalization.

Work Process

Often anthropologists are tackling issues of how to make the process of getting work done run more smoothly and efficiently. The next time you use a Xerox copy machine, notice that the start button is green. This is the result of research conducted in 1979 by anthropologist Lucy Suchman who was working at the Palo Alto Research Center, the same center that created the computer mouse. Suchman studied how people used the copy machine and discovered that complex machines with many features were difficult for people to figure out. Simplicity was at least as important as multiple features. So, now all Xerox copy machines, no matter how complex, have a single green copy button. You can walk up to any one and make a simple copy with ease. Another example is the work of Bonnie Nardi, who has worked at Hewlett-Packard, Apple, and AT&T and helped Hewlett-Packard develop a better spreadsheet. Nardi observed how spreadsheets were filled out, and she discovered that, contrary to the method engineers had imagined, one person does not fill out the entire sheet. Instead, it is passed around and different workers fill in different portions. This led to the development of a more useful, efficient spreadsheet design (Weise 1999).

Group Behavior

As specialists at people-watching, anthropologists have a great deal to contribute to all fields that strive to understand group behavior. For example, companies that want to market products to recent college graduates might benefit from asking this group of consumers: What is important to you? What is your daily life like? What are your dreams? How do you spend your time? An anthropologist was one of the researchers at PortiCo Research who went into the homes and offices of people in their twenties, met their roommates and friends, and talked to them about music, life, and goals. This information helped marketers to better understand what people in this age group want. The research, according to John McManus of Simba Information, "gives more of a human dimension to what all the quantitative [statistical] data would be telling you" (cited in Fass 2001:C11). Anthropologists' field techniques and approach to understanding human behavior are especially useful in studying marketing, consumer behavior, and product design. Anthropologists also contribute to understanding consumption in the global marketplace: how products move around the world and how they are recontextualized in each new locale.

Additionally, anthropologists study group behavior in organizational settings. As part of a multidisciplinary team that included psychologists, computer scientists, engineers, and management specialists, anthropologists participated in a study of self-managed work teams in ten companies. In self-managed work teams, the workers are organized into teams and each team manages itself. Typically, the team has no direct supervisor as the team takes on the tasks the supervisor would perform, such as dividing up their work assignments, prioritizing their work, and possibly even conducting corrective counseling with problem team members. The goal of this study was to understand what made these teams successful. While a variety of qualitative and quantitative techniques were used by all members of the research team, the use of anthropological ethnographic methods showed that while team leaders were important to team success, many factors outside of the team's control were important as well. Teams needed manager support, proper reward systems, and lots of up-front training, for example. So, this is a case in which anthropologists focused on groups, the interaction of members of each group, and each group's interaction with forces external to it (Jordan 1999).

Organizational Change

The skills of the anthropologist are also helpful in understanding organizational change. For example, when two corporations merge, they must go through substantial organizational change in order to fit together. The failure of corporate mergers can sometimes be traced to the difficulty of joining two companies that have very different cultures, value systems, and approaches to business into one unified whole. A recent anthropological study of a merger, in which employees from both former companies were employed in the new one, indicated that employees from one of the corporations were unwilling to adapt their culture and values to those of the new company. These employees felt the new corporate goals did not reflect the necessities of their business and would cause them to lose market share for their products.

Another example of organizational change comes from the work-team study mentioned above. The move from organizing employees according to a large, top-down hierarchical structure to self-managed work teams is a popular change that is considered effective for increasing a product's competitiveness in the marketplace. Teams often come up with ideas that improve the product or reduce its cost—ideas that their bosses, who are further removed from the actual work, would never have thought of. Also, teaming means a flattened organizational structure in which the position, and therefore the salary, of the first-line supervisor has been eliminated. The reduced salary costs can be passed on as a cost savings to the consumer, thereby increasing the product's competitiveness. When an organization as a whole changes from a hierarchical organizational form to a flattened work-team structure, it is as if the entire organization is turned on its side. The change has both positive and negative ramifications throughout the organization. In recent studies of this form of change, anthropologists have learned the problems that are likely to occur and can recommend the best practices to avoid these problems (Jordan 1999).

Diversity

Anthropologists who work in organizations do what they traditionally have done best—gain an understanding of cultural groupings. Organizations consist of multiple complex special-interest groups, partly because the world's workforce is diverse. In Saudi Arabia, for example, 25 percent of the population is non-Saudi and in one Riyadh hospital alone, employees hold passports from over 60 different countries (Jordan 2011). In London, one in four residents is a member of an ethnic minority group; resident communities originate from over 90 countries (Regional Language Network 2008).

The Hudson Institute, in a report commissioned by the US Department of Labor, predicted that sometime in the twenty-first century, non-Hispanic whites will no longer retain their majority status in the United States (cited in Kogod 1994:28). In 2012, the US Census Bureau reported that 16.7 percent of the population was of Hispanic or Latino origin (US Census Bureau 2012). By the year 2050, one-half of the US population will be African American, Hispanic American, Native American, and Asian American. In addition, 500,000 immigrants arrive in the United States legally every year. The United States, which has only 5 percent of the world's population, takes in almost 50 percent of the world's immigrants, excluding refugees (Fernandez 1991:5). Between 2000 and 2012 approximately 14,000,000 immigrants came to the US (SUSPS 2012). Diversity is becoming the norm in US work sites as well as in work sites around the world.

Diversity, one of the most prominent features of business culture, includes gender and ethnicity characteristics, as well as cultural groupings, such as political, religious, and sexual lifestyle affiliations. Anthropologists work to understand diversity's role and impact in organizational settings. Mark Grey (1999), for example, studied high rates of job turnover at an Iowa meatpacking plant that employs Mexican migrant workers and US Anglo supervisors. He uncovered motivations among the different groups and their effect on the rate of employee turnover.

Globalization

Business has gone global—evidenced by export/import data. According to the World Bank and the World Trade Organization, by 2008, global exports exceeded 16 trillion in US dollars, and 52 percent of the global GDP was accounted for by exports and imports (Rodrigue et al. 2009). A characteristic of complex business organizations is that the people who consume their goods or use their services, the people they employ, and the locations where they operate are culturally diverse. Employees are likely to work for companies that have offices abroad. North Americans, for example, might work for US companies that also have offices in Hong Kong, Munich, and Cairo, or they might become expats themselves and move to countries with booming economies, such as Singapore, to find work. In addition, many workers are employed by foreign-owned companies. These workers, while they work on home soil, must adjust to a set of culturally different business practices. In many situations, the companies also must adjust their business practices to the cultures of foreign locations. A leading industrial statesman in Japan remarked that the approaches and operations of US and Japanese companies are 95 percent alike but that it is the 5 percent difference that really matters (Harris and Moran 1987).

Tomoko Hamada (1991) studied the issues involved in Japanese–US business ventures. She uncovered the difficulties of a joint venture in Japan between US and Japanese corporations where everything from corporate structure to layout of the equipment on the factory floor to quality of the product had to be negotiated through two different cultural perspectives. Hedrick Serrie (1999) studied the culturally different styles of management found in China and the United States, demonstrating that what is recognized as appropriate management behavior reflects larger cultural values. In the case of China and the United States, these values are so different that success in negotiating organizational issues across such a cultural divide requires grasping and respecting the other's perspective and behavior.

Anthropologists understand that the world is not really becoming homogenized by globalization. Instead, human groups around the world express their local identities in the ways in which they recontextualize goods, services, and even people from other cultural groups. The world is a complex web of interacting and overlapping, contesting and cooperating, flexible cultural groupings. Discovering the ways consumers and employees as individuals and as groups negotiate the global impact on their local environments is a fascinating and valuable contribution of anthropologists to the study of globalization.

PLAN OF THIS BOOK

My goal is to use anthropological methods to better understand human behavior in all of its settings, from an isolated village in the Himalayas to a corporate office in New York City or Hong Kong.

Chapter 2 offers a brief overview of the history of business anthropology. Anthropologists' qualitative fieldwork techniques are some of our valuable contributions to the study of organizations, marketing, consumer behavior, and product design. In chapter 3, the basics of how anthropologists do fieldwork in these contexts are described. Chapter 4 explores some of the unique characteristics of the anthropological approach to understanding culture, the places where cultures intersect, and the ways in which humans negotiate their many identities. I provide examples to show how anthropologists use these understandings in business. In chapter 5, the ethical issues of greatest concern in business anthropology are reviewed and discussed. Anthropology's professional organizations have developed codes of ethics, which their members are expected to uphold.

Work in business anthropology is varied, but to give it some order, I divide it into the following three overlapping subject areas or subfields: (1) marketing and consumer behavior, (2) product design, and (3) organizational anthropology. Chapter 6 describes work that anthropologists have conducted in the fields of marketing and consumer behavior, where our methods allow us to get close to consumers and learn their needs. Anthropology's theoretical perspectives allow us to understand how consumption plays out on the world stage. Chapter 7 takes us into the fields of product design and development, where we see how anthropological methods contribute to a more acute awareness of how the design of a product contributes to meeting consumers' needs. In this chapter we also see how anthropology's theoretical background allows us to then place our knowledge of end-user behavior in the context of the social and cultural complexities of the consumers' world. Chapter 8 looks at organizational anthropology, noting the wide variety of types of organizations anthropologists study. The chapter contains specific examples of how an anthropologist works in an organization as a consultant to solve organizational problems. Chapter 9 focuses on a phenomenon that is significant to all subfields of business anthropology:

globalization. It provides examples of the work anthropologists are doing in global business; since globalization crosscuts the three afore-mentioned fields, some examples also appear in the earlier chapters.

While much of anthropologically based research done in and for organizations never mentions the word *culture*, it still involves using anthropological theories and methods to understand an array of problems in organizational work and everyday life. One of anthropologists' great strengths is a holistic perspective, by which I mean the ability to understand the big picture. When business anthropologists are asked to answer a specific question, they characteristically pull back from the specific area of study to figure out how that question is embedded in other larger questions. Chapter 10 explains this technique and provides examples. In chapter 11, we look at the future—the world in which we live will continue to become smaller, with nations becoming even more dependent on each other for goods and services. In this dynamic world, anthropology will always have a vital role to play.

Chapter Two

A History of Anthropology in Western Organizational Life

We've always been in business . . .

A friend who is an industrial psychologist once introduced me to some business associates as an anthropologist who worked in businesses. He further explained that I also had worked in an exotic setting: I worked with North American contemporary covens of witches. For an anthropologist, however, working with witches is normal; it is working in business that is exotic! In the last three decades, however, we have experienced phenomenal growth in anthropological work in organizations. Actually, this is a rebirth of interest, as anthropology has a long history of work in business organizations (Baba 1986; Gamst 1977; Schwartzman 1993).

INDUSTRIAL ANTHROPOLOGY AND THE HUMAN RELATIONS SCHOOL, 1930–1960

To tell the story of this history, I must begin in Chicago. By the 1870s, Chicago was a city bursting with energy; it was the world's largest grain, livestock, and lumber market. Volatile Chicago was the gateway to the West and the site of the 1893 World's Fair. Workers from the southern states as well as from Europe flooded into Chicago to find jobs. Chicago was a bustling city of great wealth and great poverty. In 1886, a worker demonstration publicizing the need for an eight-hour workday ended in violence with an exploding bomb and shootings; police and demonstrators died. By protesting working and living conditions, Chicago's laborers would help initiate the formation of the organized labor movements. In 1889, Jane Addams founded Hull House, an early settlement house aimed at improving conditions in the slums. This was one of the first efforts in the United States to recognize and solve urban poverty.

By the 1920s, Chicago was a center for crime and creativity. It was famous for gangsters, speakeasies, and mob warfare, including the 1929 St. Valentine's Day Massacre. It was also famous for the many artists who lived there, including writers Carl Sandburg and Upton Sinclair and musician Louis Armstrong. Sandburg immortalized the city in his poem "Chicago":

> Hog Butcher for the World,
> Tool Maker, Stacker of Wheat,
> Player with Railroads and the Nation's Freight Handler;
> Stormy, husky, brawling,
> City of the Big Shoulders.

Chicago was a center of intellectual activity as well. In 1892, the University of Chicago opened its doors. It housed the first sociology department in a US university, and in 1929, a separate department of anthropology was established. From World War I into the 1930s, sociologists and anthropologists at the University of Chicago conducted a series of studies that pioneered modern urban studies.

Between 1924 and 1933, Chicago was the location for possibly the most famous human relations study in a business setting in all of North American organizational research. Through a collaboration that ultimately involved Western Electric (the company that, as the manufacturing arm of Bell Telephone, supplied equipment to AT&T for over 100 years), the National Academy of Sciences, and Harvard School of Business Administration, a research project was conducted from 1927 to 1932 at Western Electric's Hawthorne Works, a manufacturing plant in Chicago. Early research there led to the discovery that when scientists are measuring or recording the behavior of human subjects, subjects may change their behavior because they know they are being studied, rather than because of any manipulation of the environment the scientists undertake. A change in behavior based on knowledge that one is the subject of a research study is known as the *Hawthorne Effect.*

The story of this discovery begins when Elton Mayo, an Australian psychiatrist, became director of a project to explore reasons for change in levels of productivity. In 1931, W. Lloyd Warner, an American anthropologist, whose previous research with the Murngin Aborigines of Australia had been well received, joined the project. Warner conducted research in the Bank Wiring Room at Hawthorne Works using anthropological research techniques and the functionalist theory of Malinowski and Radcliffe-Brown (functionalist theory was described briefly in the introduction). The researchers observed and recorded employee interactions while they worked. The researchers found that no matter what the manipulation of physical and management-centered stimuli, worker productivity increased. The increase was a consequence of management's interest in the workers, demonstrated by the presence of researchers like Warner. The workers' response is an example of the Hawthorne Effect.

These researchers conducted the first qualitative study of informal social organization in the work setting. The Hawthorne Studies and Warner's anthropological contribution to them were seminal to the realization by organizational scientists that understanding human relations was crucial to understanding organizations and worker productivity. This realization led to the creation of *human relations* as a field of study. The field of business anthropology, known then as industrial anthropology, was born.

The downturn in the North American economy during the Depression brought an end to the Hawthorne Studies, and little anthropology was conducted in business settings during the 1930s. Organizational research rebounded with the revival of the economy during World War II. Chicago continued to be the center of the human relations school. The Committee on Human Relations in Industry was organized at the University of Chicago and was supported by important businesses of the time, such as Sears, Roebuck and Co.; Container Corporation of America; and Libby, McNeill, & Libby. Warner eventually became chairman of the committee, which also involved other early applied anthropologists such as Burleigh Gardner (see Gardner 1978).

Former students of Warner at Harvard, Conrad Arensberg and Eliot Chapple, began working in industrial anthropology. Arensberg, Chapple, and other industrial anthropologists at Harvard formed the Society for Applied Anthropology (SfAA) in 1941, the largest and oldest professional association of applied anthropologists existing today. The journal, *Applied Anthropology*, which they founded as the publication of the SfAA, published many studies of organizational life. Now called *Human Organization*, this journal is the leading North American journal of applied anthropology.

During the 1940s, anthropologists who were trained by the Harvard and Chicago groups conducted numerous studies and spread the specialty of industrial anthropology to universities around North America. This work in the 1940s continued to reflect the functionalist theoretical paradigm. Methodologically, the work combined both qualitative and quantitative approaches. Chapple and Arensberg developed *interactional analysis,* a technique for quantifying interactive human behavior through specific measurements of interactions. Case studies, for example an in-depth look at a single business, were the predominant data-gathering approach.

Arensberg studied teamwork and productivity in a shoe factory. William F. Whyte, a student of Arensberg, Chapple, and Warner, studied the interrelations of supervisors, waitresses, cooks, and customers in local restaurants in Chicago. He later wrote a seminal book, *Men at Work* (1961), that included studies of the restaurant, hotel, steel, automobile, glass, and petroleum industries. Burleigh Gardner, with Whyte (1945), studied first-line supervisors, the men caught in the middle between assembly-line workers and higher management. Gardner (1949) also published a textbook on human relations that was important in the field for many years. Other studies include ones about technology change on an assembly line at IBM's Endicott plant (Richardson and Walker 1948), the incentive system at Bundy Tubing (Whyte 1948), leadership and change in Eastern Corporation's Lakeshore Mill (Sayles 1952), industrial rate busters (Dalton 1948), work and informal relations on an automotive assembly line (Walker and Guest 1952), and a strike at Chicago's Inland Steel Container Company (Whyte 1951). Meanwhile, in Britain, anthropologists from the Manchester school of social anthropology were studying work on the shop floor (van Marrewijk 2010).

In 1946, Gardner and Warner stepped out of the university atmosphere to become business entrepreneurs themselves. Along with William Henry, a clinical psychologist, they formed Social Research, Incorporated, a management consulting firm. This was the first management consulting firm run by anthropologists who used anthropological techniques and theory to analyze problems in organizations and tackle questions about consumer behavior. The firm would eventually add sociologists and others with interdisciplinary degrees. Among this firm's projects were: developing a system of employee attitude surveys for Sears, Roebuck and Co.; identifying, for a chain of drugstores, why their pharmacists had such poor morale; creating a training and development program for department heads of a large hospital; and conducting research for Alka-Seltzer, which showed that people tend to be either "headachers" or "stomachachers" and that advertisements needed to reach both populations. The long life of this consulting firm and its many significant projects are a testament to the vitality of industrial anthropology. The work they conducted included all the subfields of business anthropology mentioned in the introduction to this book: (1) marketing and consumer behavior, (2) design anthropology, and (3) organizational anthropology.

The impact of the Hawthorne Study is still felt not only in organizational studies but also in all of social science. In organizational studies, the findings of the Hawthorne Study documented that productivity and performance would increase if managers were more concerned with the human side of their workers and practiced more humanizing treatment. Worker satisfaction and morale became central concerns. Humans were not robots after all. There were problems, however, with the Hawthorne research, one being that humanizing variables were difficult to measure. The Hawthorne Study and the human relations school eventually fell under severe criticism. Critics of the Hawthorne research demonstrated that many of the findings of the study could not be tied to measurable variables like economic incentives and corrective discipline (Franke and Kaul 1978).

Functionalist theory also was proving inadequate. As mentioned previously, the basic idea of functionalist theory is that social phenomena are present in an organization because they serve a function in that organization and if they did not, they would not be there. This theoretical approach does not allow for tension, conflict, or dissidence. The human relations school, with functionalism as its paradigm, could not explain or understand many of the real issues of business organizations. There was no room in the theory for strife and conflicts of power. Labor disputes, strikes, and the rise of labor unions could not be accounted for in this theoretical paradigm, and the human relations school was criticized for ignoring labor unions.

New paradigms began to emerge in organization studies that took into account the environment and power differentials.

While theory in the general field of anthropology was changing, and theoretical approaches like Julian Steward's cultural ecology, mentioned earlier, could have brought significant insights into organizational studies, the anthropologists studying organizations remained loyal to functionalism. Their influence, like the human relations school as a whole, began to wane around 1960. The contributions of the human relations school are important, however. Functionalism is useful when tempered with an understanding of its limitations and when augmented with other theoretical stances, such as materialism, or even postmodernism.

Possibly the most important contribution of the human relations school was the appreciation of the informal structure in organizations. Organizations leave a lengthy paper trail of their formal organization structure; examples are the organization chart (a diagram that shows each job position in the organization and to whom the person in that position reports) and written policies and job descriptions (the formalized ways of behaving that are legitimized and publicly stated by the holders of authority). Equally important, however, are the structure and ways of behaving that are not written down or expressed in organizationally sanctioned ways. These informal patterns in the organization are outside the control of formal structure and are key to understanding the organization. It is the human relations school that gave us the concept of *informal organization* (Gamst 1977).

In the 1950s, another anthropologist was beginning a career that would be highly influential in business. From 1950 to 1955, Edward T. Hall served as director of the US State Department's "Point Four" training program, designed to teach technicians who would be working outside North America about cross-cultural communication. Hall understood the significance of the failure to communicate effectively due to cultural differences. He built a career in the field and eventually wrote several seminal works well-known in business, anthropology, communication, and many other fields.

In his first book, *The Silent Language*, Hall explained culture as communication and communication as involving much more than just language. Communication also included nonverbal characteristics and had to be understood in cultural context. In later books he explored the culturally different ways of conceiving space and time. Hall's influence in the fields of intercultural communication and intercultural training has been monumental. Hall understood that errors in cross-cultural communication could destroy a business deal or a peace agreement. His work was recognized for its theoretical impact and international value, and he continued to contribute to cross-cultural business through the remainder of the twentieth century (Baba 1995: 117–118). Other anthropologists, like Gary Ferraro, have continued Hall's work on communication in international settings (Ferraro 2002).

THE ETHICS QUESTIONS, 1960–1980

The period of the 1960s was the time of love beads, Volkswagen buses painted in flowers, bell-bottom pants, the Beatles, free love, and easy drugs. Bob Dylan was defining the morals of a generation in his music, and North American youth were determined never to trust anyone over the age of 30. It was a time of moral reckoning with mass demonstrations for civil rights and against the Vietnam War. Young US men were fleeing to Canada to avoid being drafted, and students were demonstrating on campuses all over North America. It was a time of violence with the assassinations of John Kennedy, Martin Luther King Jr., and Robert Kennedy.

During this volatile period of great creativity and destruction, a set of events occurred in the anthropological community that effectively closed anthropology to consulting work and severely impacted organizational research by professional anthropologists. The US Department of the Army initiated a research project to hire social scientists, including anthropologists, to work in Latin America. This project was designed to provide the army with information that would assist it in dealing with internal revolutions in Latin American countries. Called

Project Camelot, it had a budget of some $6 million. Before the project could get underway, a Chilean newspaper learned of it and began a vigorous protest, which reverberated throughout Latin America. The US Congress and the army canceled the project. However, the possibility that anthropologists might have engaged in secret research for the US government, which meant informing on the Latin American people, sent shock waves through the profession. Anthropologists have always considered it their first responsibility not to harm the people they study. Many felt that had anthropologists participated in Project Camelot, they would have been acting in a professionally unethical manner by "informing" on the subjects of their research, the Latin Americans.

Another incident occurred in 1968 when a job advertisement was published by the American Anthropological Association (AAA). The US government was seeking an anthropologist to work with its Psychological Operations Headquarters in Vietnam. The research conducted would be to evaluate "enemy" propaganda and US counterpropaganda on a "target audience." The job was viewed by many in the anthropological community as directly tied to US intervention in Vietnam. That suggested to them that the anthropologist hired would be conducting clandestine research among the Vietnamese people, which would then be used by the US military. Assumably this research would be classified, remaining secret from the anthropological community. The membership of the AAA was again in an uproar and removed the job advertisement from its listings. In 1970, information came to light that anthropologists had conducted war-related research in Thailand from 1967 to 1969. Again, members of the association were enraged. At the height of the sentiments opposing the US military involvement in Southeast Asia, many felt that this aiding of the US military was harmful to the Southeast Asian people and was, therefore, unethical behavior for an anthropologist.

The suspicion concerning the ethics of the projects described above was widespread in the anthropological community (Fluehr-Lobban 1991). The AAA condemned "clandestine" or "secret" research on grounds that there was some evidence that anthropological research had been connected with counterinsurgency activity. In 1971, the membership adopted the Principles of Professional Responsibility, which stated that "no reports should be provided to sponsors that are not available to the general public. . . . The anthropologist . . . should enter into no secret agreement with the sponsor regarding the research, the results or the final report." This statement in the profession's code of ethics effectively prevented anthropologists from working as business consultants or in research positions in corporations.

Corporate leadership typically restricts the publication of reports prepared for them in order to protect the corporation and prevent others from gaining a competitive edge. While such corporate work is not related to counterinsurgency and clandestine government operations, the ethical code designed to prevent participation in counterinsurgency operations closed the door on proprietary research in organizations as well. Through the 1960s and the 1970s, little research was conducted in or for business organizations.

THE REBIRTH OF BUSINESS ANTHROPOLOGY, 1980 AND BEYOND

By the 1980s, large numbers of anthropologists were working in applied fields in a wide variety of contexts unrelated to counterinsurgency. The profession once again entered into intense debates over ethics. As a result, the AAA decided to allow proprietary research and thus legitimated the contractual work many anthropologists were beginning to perform as consultants. At the same time, business leaders and the popular press took a sudden interest in subjects about which anthropologists have expertise. The term *culture* became popular in the 1980s. On the surface it appeared that this clamor among business analysts regarding culture in organizations was largely a result of the American response to Japanese business success. Four best-selling business books fed this interest. In 1981, William Ouchi published *Theory Z*, and Richard Pascale and Anthony Athos published *The Art of Japanese Management*—books addressing the role of culture in Japanese business success. The following year Terrence Deal and Allan Kennedy published *Corporate Cultures,* and Thomas Peters and Robert Waterman published *In Search of Excellence*—books bringing home to North Americans the notion that successful businesses must be concerned with their organizational cultures.

While some work had already appeared in this fledgling field (for example, Hofstead 1980), it was the four best sellers mentioned above that contributed the most toward publicizing and popularizing the culture concept and thus attracted the interest of the business community. After the term *corporate culture* experienced an initial period of favor in the popular press, the term *organizational culture* settled into consulting and academia to describe one more construct to use in studying organizations. In management consulting from the business-training perspective, organizational culture is seen as additive, one more piece of the organization. Throughout the 1980s, management interest in anthropology focused on methodology. This interest was reflected in several publications in management journals by anthropologists, like N. C. Morey and F. Luthans's (1984) article "An Emic Perspective and Ethnoscience Methods for Organizational Research," published in the *Academy of Management Review,* as well as in publications, such as

Helen Schwartzman's (1993) *Ethnography in Organizations,* in Sage Publications' Qualitative Research Methods Series.

The 1980s research took several forms. Some of it was found in the study of work; the Society for the Anthropology of Work and its *Anthropology of Work Review* published research on work across different cultures (Applebaum 1984; Sachs 1989). Gerald Britan and Ronald Cohen (1980), however, set the stage for a new field of organizational anthropology in their article "Toward an Anthropology of Formal Organizations." Britan and Frank Dubinskas renewed the tradition of industrial ethnography; Gerald Britan (1981) conducted an ethnographic study of the Experimental Technology Incentives Program of the Department of Commerce, and Dubinskas (1988) edited a volume of ethnographies of high-tech corporations.

The rise of Japan as a powerful economic player and the increasing globalization of business created a new concern with understanding economics and culture around the world. Anthropologists worked in the field of international business consulting. Vern Terpstra and Kenneth David (1985) coauthored a text on international business. Tomoko Hamada (1991) conducted extensive research on American and Japanese organizational and cultural interactions. Others worked in the field of intercultural training (Ojile 1986). Work on the dynamics of formal organizations began appearing (Jordan 1990). Marietta Baba (1989) studied the development of local knowledge systems among workers. Jeanne Connors and Thomas Romberg (1991) analyzed manager reactions to quality-control programs. Other anthropologists, such as Elizabeth Briody, were employed by corporations to conduct in-house research, the results of which were published in anthropological journals (Briody and Baba 1991; Briody and Chrisman 1991).

The *Anthropology of Work Review* published a special issue on organizational culture, and several other edited collections on organizational culture and cross-cultural management appeared (Hamada and Jordan 1990; Sachs 1989; Serrie 1986; Sibley and Hamada 1994). The surge of interest in organizations by anthropologists in the 1980s was tied to the surge of interest in anthropology by organizational behaviorists. The possibility for cross-fertilization was great (Jordan 1989; Walck and Jordan 1993). Additionally in the 1980s, anthropologists like Steve Barnet inspired others to consider consumer research. He not only had a successful consulting business but he wrote a column for *Advertizing Age,* a trade periodical, in which he tackled issues about cultural differences and the importance of symbols and meanings. Those he impacted include Patricia Sunderland, Rita Denny, and Timothy Malefyt who all became important in anthropology's contribution to consumer behavior and product design (Sunderland and Denny 2007:30).

In 1987, the Institute for Research on Learning (IRL), which was funded from a variety of sources including the Xerox Foundation, was founded. The task of this institute was to find solutions to the crisis in learning that was outlined in the federally commissioned report *A Nation at Risk*. That report stated the United States would be left behind if it did not significantly improve the quality of learning in its schools and workplaces. The mission of IRL was to pursue research aimed at understanding the nature of learning in all settings and to use this research to create new, more-effective learning environments. While the work at IRL was purposefully interdisciplinary, drawing from fields like economics, statistics, psychology, and computer science, it was heavily influenced by anthropology from the beginning. The research methods were anthropological, including participant observation, ethnographic interviewing, and interaction analysis. The reason for the emphasis on anthropological techniques was simple: the researchers at IRL were committed to the notion that to understand learning, they must watch people in the act of learning, whether in schools or in workplaces. The techniques of anthropology allowed them to do this.

The theoretical paradigm on which IRL work was based was the notion that learning does not occur in a passive situation where an instructor places knowledge in the head of a student. Instead, learning occurs in social situations of meaning, communities of practice where knowledge is socially constructed. Anthropologists Brigitte Jordan, Patricia Sachs, Shelly Goldman, and others were involved in this work. They looked at ways to redesign work spaces to better facilitate work and ways that workers as members of learning communities interact with larger organizational units; additionally, they figured out how an organization "knows" what it knows.

The research at IRL has had influence far beyond the individual projects conducted and has impacted anthropology and our understanding of how humans learn. This research included the work practices of claims processors at an insurance company, of workers in the communications and control center of an airline's ground operations, and of technicians who repair copy machines. The analysis provided insights into ways to improve work performance by increasing learning of key information. The work attracted attention in the fields of marketing, consumer behavior, and product design and was instrumental in anthropologists becoming involved in those fields.

In the 1980s, anthropology's influence in business schools began to grow. Anthropologists teaching in business schools have played a critical role in the development of consumer studies in both their business school teaching environments and their discipline of anthropology. Grant McCracken—Massachusetts Institute of Technology, John F. Sherry—Notre Dame, Eric Arnould—the University of Bath, UK, Barbara Olsen—State University of New York-Old Westbury, Janeen Costa—University of Utah, and Annamma Joy—University of British Columbia are just a few of the anthropologists who have impacted the business school community. In addition, business school faculty like Ron Hill and Carol Kaufman-Scarborough, who received their training from schools of business, are using ethnography in their data gathering (Arnould 2001). Consumer behavior consultants like Paco Underhill have appropriated anthropological techniques for use in their work. Today, consulting in marketing and consumer behavior is one of the fastest-growing job markets for anthropologists.

In the 1990s, anthropologists moved into the field of design. The anthropologists at Xerox were influential in the adoption of ethnographic techniques in this field. Lucy Suchman was project leader on a project for which the Palo Alto Research Center collaborated with the Doblin Group, an innovative design consulting firm. Rick Robinson, head of research at the Doblin Group, was so impressed with the value of ethnography that, along with two other Doblin employees, he left Doblin and started E-Lab in 1994. The premise at E-Lab was that all design projects would be grounded in ethnographic research. This was E-Lab's competitive edge. A number of anthropologists worked at E-Lab and Sapient, the firm Robinson subsequently joined.

Though not an anthropologist, Robinson has done much to publicize and spread the use of ethnography in the product design and development fields (Wasson 2000). Sapient employed 23 PhDs in anthropology and closely aligned disciplines, and an additional 100 people in its offices around the world were using ethnographic techniques. Ethnography became the fashionable research tool for other well-known consulting and design firms, such as Scient, Viant, and Razorfish, who employed anthropologists to conduct research on new product designs. Corporations hiring anthropologists in-house included Xerox, with nine PhD anthropologists, General Motors, Kodak, Motorola, and Hewlett Packard (Cefkin 2009). In the Netherlands, Hans Tennekes, Willem Koot, and others were establishing the field of business anthropology in organization studies, while in the UK Paul Bates was defining the difference between the anthropological perspective on organizations and that of other organization specialists. In France, Jean François Chanlet was publishing articles on the multiple layers of culture in organizations (van Marrewijk 2010).

In the last decade, the fields of business anthropology have further crystallized and grown. In the 2000s, Intel employed 15 PhD anthropologists, while Microsoft employed seven (Cefkin 2009; Fitzgerald 2006). The members of the popular press have periodically released articles on anthropology in corporations that suggest anthropologists are at the cutting edge of research. For example, CNNMoney.com (Copeland 2010) released a story about Genevieve Bell at Intel, positioning her as the exotic corporate rock star who dresses in black and "learned to kill things" during her childhood in an aboriginal Australian community. She now helps Intel enter new markets through her research on how people around the world use computers and phones (Jordan and Caulkins 2013). New books in business anthropology continue to appear, including Briody, Trotter, and Meerwarth's (2010) volume on General Motors, Krause Jensen's (2010) work on the electronics company Bang and Olufsen, Røyrvik's (2011) study of managerial ideology in a Norwegian oil company, Caulkins and Jordan's (2012) edited collection on topics in organizational anthropology, and Malefyt and Morais's (2012) volume on advertising.

In 2005 Eric Arnould and Craig Thompson published a seminal article in the *Journal of Consumer Research* in which they reviewed 20 years of consumer research, identified a research tradition that they called consumer culture theory (CCT), and explained how this research studied the cultural dimensions of the consumption cycle. Arnould and John Sherry were then instrumental in developing the CCT Conference, first held at University of Notre Dame in 2006. At this annual conference the papers and posters reflect the CCT approach, which "considers consumption and its involved behavioral choices and practices as social and cultural phenomena" (Consumer Culture Theory 2011). Most of the scientists attending and presenting at this conference teach in business schools and are committed to understanding the cultural meanings of consumer behavior. The conference draws presenters from around the world; the August 2012 conference was held at Oxford University in the UK. The conference has helped shape this new field of consumer culture theory in marketing.

In addition, important new books have been published such as Patricia Sunderland and Rita Denny's *Doing Anthropology in Consumer Research* (2007) in which they give detailed examples of their work as cultural analysts who consult on consumer behavior. They provide theoretical background and explanations of the research steps for a variety of client projects they have conducted over the years. Another contribution is Timothy Malefyt and Brian Moeran's (2003) edited collection of case studies by anthropologists working in consumer behavior.

Design firms are hungry for anthropologists and their approaches, and the field of design anthropology has grown exponentially in the last 15 years. In design anthropology, a significant conference similar to the CCT Conference is the Ethnographic Praxis in Industry Conference (EPIC), born in 2005 and held for the eighth time in Savannah, Georgia, in 2012. This conference was started by a group of anthropologists that include Ken Anderson at Intel, Tracey Lovejoy at Microsoft, Jeanette Blomberg at IBM, and Christina Wasson at University of North Texas. Goals for EPIC include "to promote public recognition of practicing ethnography as a profession and to support the continuing professionalization of the field" (http://epiconference.com).

EPIC has defined and crystallized the field. It is attended by design anthropologists, designers, and others in industry and in design firms who use ethnographic techniques to develop new product ideas. At the 2009 conference in Chicago, for example, multiple local design firms participated in showcasing anthropological (ethnographic) techniques. Publications in this field are growing with EPIC's proceedings published annually by the American Anthropological Association, and with other works like Patricia Sunderland and Rita Denny's previously mentioned 2007 book. The field is an exciting example of the multidisciplinary collaboration of anthropologists, designers, and others interested in this approach to product design. Recently EPIC has expanded to include presentations on work process design and other topics in organizational anthropology.

The interest in business anthropology is global as the International Union of Anthropological and Ethnological Sciences now includes the Commission on Enterprise Anthropology headed by Tomoko Hamada Connolly and Zhang Jijiao, and in addition to the US and European countries, business anthropology conferences are being held in Japan (International Forum on Business and Anthropology, Museum of Ethnology, Osaka, 2010) and China (International Union of Anthropological and Ethnological Sciences Commission on Enterprise Anthropology, 2009 and 2011, and First International Conference of Business Anthropology, China, 2012). A further sign of the maturity of the field and its international nature is the birth of two journals of Business Anthropology. *The International Journal of Business Anthropology* sponsored by the University of Sun Yat-Sen, China, and VU University, Amsterdam, is the result of the work of Robert Tian and published its initial issue in 2010. *The Journal of Business Anthropology*, an open access journal hosted by the Copenhagen Business School, published its first issue in 2011 and is the result of the efforts of Brian Moeran and Christina Garsten (Moeran and Garsten 2011).

CONCLUSION

Work on and for business has been a part of anthropology since the early decades of the twentieth century. Through the 1990s and into the twenty-first century, growth in the field of business anthropology has continued to explode globally. Anthropologists work in consulting firms and corporate research departments as well as academic institutions. Universities are offering graduate degrees in business anthropology.[1] For the most part the work is marked by the use of ethnographic methods and a holistic perspective. When studying consumer behavior, anthropologists understand that the product user is their primary unit of study. Human behavior must always be studied in context; to find what consumers want, one must ask *and* observe them. When studying the organization itself, anthropologists realize that organizational structure and group behavior and values must be understood in order to formulate a description of and subsequent conclusions about the workings of the organization. The words of Burleigh Gardner, after some 30 years of work in Social Research, Incorporated, are apropos.

> I feel that training as a social anthropologist provides a valuable basic orientation. The emphasis on social structure and on the interrelations of all activities and cultural artifacts into a social system provides the conceptual basis for examining the wide range of people problems with which business must deal. (Gardner 1978:259)

In later chapters of this book, I will discuss many examples of the work anthropologists have conducted in and for business over the past several decades.

Endnote

[1] For example, among those offering graduate programs in business anthropology are the University of North Texas, Oregon State University, and Wayne State University in the US; University of Copenhagen in Denmark; Shantou University in China; and Swinburne University in Australia.

Chapter Three

Techniques for Conducting Fieldwork for Business Organizations

*What is an anthropologist doing on the
assembly line and in the high-rise executive suite?*

Anthropology as a field of study began in the mid-nineteenth century as scientists in Europe and the United States struggled to understand behavior in non-Western societies. The goal of anthropology then and now is to understand why humans behave as they do, what in their behavior is panhuman and therefore natural to the species, what in their behavior is unique to a specific group and therefore cultural, and how human practices worldwide can be explained. This goal requires the study of human behavior in natural settings, which we refer to as the "field" (Walck and Jordan 1993).

Much of the uniqueness of the anthropological worldview is both a cause and a consequence of the process of gathering data in unfamiliar settings. Knowing nothing about the Trobriand islanders, for example, forces the anthropologist to go to the natural setting and meet with Trobrianders in order to learn about them firsthand. Prior to Malinowski's (1981 [1922]) study in the Trobriands, there was no thorough anthropological information available and no way to gather it from a distance. Roger and Felix Keesing explain:

> Whether the setting is city, town, village, or jungle hut, the mode of
> anthropological research is in many important respects the same.
> Most essential, it entails a deep immersion into the life of a peo-

ple . . . . [The anthropologist] learns their language and tries to learn their mode of life. . . . His place and his task are in many ways like those of an infant. He does not understand the noises, the visual images, the smells, that carry rich meanings for those around him . . . . He can administer questionnaires to find out about the world he has entered little better than an infant can, and for many of the same reasons: he does not know what the questions are that have answers. (Keesing and Keesing 1971:12–13)

Ethnographic techniques were devised to cope with the field setting, where every pattern was hidden and every experience unfamiliar. Fieldwork in such a setting is different from fieldwork in a setting in one's own culture. Yet, the strength of using ethnographic techniques in a familiar setting is that they challenge the anthropologist's assumptions. By guiding anthropologists to learn cultural patterns anew, the techniques help them delve below the obvious cultural familiarities. Francisco Aguilera, an anthropologist who has been doing business consulting for 25 years, explained that anthropologists have the ability to begin their data gathering as an unbounded inquiry with no preconceived notion of what is important (Aguilera 1996). They have to discover the questions to ask as well as the answers.

Anthropology's qualitative fieldwork techniques, discussed in this chapter, are one of its most valuable contributions to business. Recognizing the value of anthropological techniques, researchers in many other disciplines now make use of them in their work. We will now explore some of the information-gathering techniques that anthropologists use.

OBSERVATION

Participant observation is the gathering of data about the daily life and customs of a people while participating, to the extent possible, in that life. This was the preferred approach to observation used by anthropologists studying unfamiliar cultures. We use it in business as well. In some cases, it is not appropriate to participate in the observed activities. Then the anthropologist observes and records the behavior. I begin using my anthropological observation skills the minute I arrive at the work site of the organization I am studying.

If the site has a parking lot, for example, I notice the size and percent of occupancy of the lot. I notice if there are reserved parking spaces and, if so, for whom they are reserved. I notice the locations of outdoor gathering areas, whether there might be picnic tables for lunch or an area where employees gather to smoke. From these observations, I have learned potentially useful information about the organization before I ever enter the building. Reserved parking spaces for executives and various levels of managers, for example, may give me some clues about the hierarchical nature of the organization. The degree of rigidity of the hierarchy may impact successful completion of some kinds of work. Amenities for employees, such as picnic tables, a designated smoking area, or a basketball court, may indicate an attempt to provide workers with extra perks to improve the quality of their experience at the workplace and may impact the relationship between employees and executives. Noting the presence of these fixtures in and around the parking area does not allow me to jump to conclusions about what they mean. Since I am like the infant who does not know what questions to ask, I cannot jump to conclusions. These kinds of details, however, are clues that may be useful later.

I continue my observations as I move into the interior of the building. I once studied a corporation that had recently undergone a merger. While the change was officially a merging of two companies, a tour of the corporate offices told me quickly to what degree the companies had merged. In this corporation's high-rise offices, each function was located on a different floor—for example, sales was on the third floor and marketing was on the fourth. Each floor was divided in half so that the sales force for one of the pre-merger companies was at the west end of the third floor and the sales force for the other pre-merger company was at the east end. This floor design occurred with each function so that, while the two pre-merger companies occupied the same building, the functional units did not appear to be merged. Before asking even a single question, my observation of the building provided me with these potential clues, and indeed it turned out that the two pre-merger companies continued to be run separately.

When I am studying consumers I use the same attention to detail. Again, our habit of treating the familiar as unfamiliar gives us the ability to see characteristics of consumer behavior that might otherwise go unnoticed. In this form of research, my field site could be an office, a home, a playground, a shopping center, or anywhere consumers are found. If I am researching the utility of a product for the home, I visit consumers in their homes and observe how they use the product. Why can we all laugh knowingly at the frustration of a parent trying to assemble a child's bicycle on Christmas Eve, only to find the instructions impossible to follow? Or a new computer user learning a supposedly "user-friendly" software program? Couldn't the directions be just a little bit clearer? My job as the anthropologist is to watch normal people navigate the learning curve of that new computer program. The designers of the equipment and writers of the instructions cannot easily guess in advance which parts of the instructions will be confusing to someone who has no familiarity with the product. By watching the user struggle, the anthropologist can provide information for better designing the program or the bicycle and the accompanying instructions. In this kind of research, it is preferable to videotape the consumer's behavior. Analyzing the tape later allows the anthropologist to study the problems in more detail.

As Rita Denny has explained, when studying consumption, being a participant observer can lead to more participation than one bargained for. In consulting for an advertising agency that was trying to get the Domino's Pizza account, she studied pizza consumption in the home and discovered that any researcher present when pizza was ordered would be expected to join in and eat pizza when it arrived! Understanding the way we consume pizza included understanding the norms of sharing pizza. Similarly, in a study of the behavior of Christmas shoppers, she created a panel of shoppers to meet together on repeated occasions and discuss their consumption practices and the meaning of Christmas shopping. She found that in this context, the panel members shared information with her about gifts they thought *she* might want to buy and traded information with each other. Again, she was drawn into a more participatory role than she had anticipated (Denny 2002).

Julian Orr used observation to understand the work process of technicians servicing copy machines. He learned that the written instructions the company provided for repair technicians to use in fixing machine problems were inadequate. He observed two technicians fixing a particularly complex problem and learned that the process they used to solve the problem involved telling each other stories about prior problems they had encountered and solved that were related to this problem. In so doing, they eventually found a solution that worked. Months later at lunch, the technicians retold the story of this particularly difficult service call to other technicians, an event Orr also observed. In observing these problem-solving behaviors, Orr was able to document the process of solving the problem and the importance of the interaction of the two technicians and their storytelling. At a later time, if asked to describe how they solved the problem, neither technician would have remembered the details of the situation as they occurred (Orr 1990).

Pierre Bourdieu distinguished between *modus operandi* and *opus operatum* (Bourdieu 1977; Brown and Duguid 1991): the former refers to the way a task looks to someone in the process of working on it, and the latter is the way a task looks to that individual when looking back on it after it is completed. In the latter, one tends to focus on the task alone and not recall the complex process one went through to accomplish the task.

Thus, the anthropologist who is observing the process of task completion must record all the details of the process, which will not be easily recalled by the participants afterward. This is invaluable in understanding work processes or, for that matter, purchasing behavior or consumption behavior.

Orr was able to give specific advice for the training of technicians and for repair guidelines as a result of his observation. His observation of the technicians' telling of the story at lunch proved valuable in another way as well. He was able to see how technicians use storytelling to create a collective memory. All those who heard the story were then able to put the solution to work when they were fixing machines. Using observation to uncover valuable insights like Orr's is not as easy as it seems, however. Orr collected many audiotapes of these events and conducted painstaking analyses of the transcripts of the tapes to document and develop his insights.

INTERVIEWING

Interviewing is a basic anthropological technique that is used in most if not all anthropological studies of organizations and consumers. There are several types of interviews that anthropologists use, including the *highly structured interview,* in which all interviewees are asked the same set of questions, and the *informal interview,* which occurs during participant observation when one is asking about the work being observed or the product being used.

In a study of work teams across ten organizations, the first step my colleagues and I took in conducting our study was to interview organization members to learn about them, their work, and their concerns (Jordan 1999). We began with the traditional anthropological premise that we did not know the right questions to ask. We wanted to get the individuals in the organizations talking so that we could learn what issues were important to them. Each team member and the managers in the management chain above the team were interviewed using a *loosely structured interview,* in which all interviewees were asked to talk about the same list of topics.

Each individual was asked about six topic areas and was encouraged to talk at length about life in the organization and on the team. The six topics discussed in the initial interviews were (1) career history, (2) company history, (3) teaming process, (4) content of team's work, (5) personal definition of successful leader and team, and (6) perceptions of advantages and disadvantages of teams. From these interviews, which ranged in length from 30 minutes to three hours with the average length being one and one-half hours, we were able to gain descriptive data about the work and structure of the teams. We were also able to learn what the team members and managers considered to be issues in teaming and team success. We could not have known in advance how they would define the issues and what those issues would be.

Another interview type is designed to allow the anthropologist to use a *content analysis* technique. This is a technique for looking at the categories people use, the meanings of these categories, and the behavior choices considered appropriate with regard to these categories. Because reality is infinite and the human mind is finite, humans group the infinite stimuli they receive into categories in order to function. These categories reflect people's perceptions of similarities and of differences or contrasts in stimuli.

There is usually more than one way to categorize stimuli. Color terms exemplify this. In English we use the terms *purple, blue, green, yellow, orange,* and *red*. However, the color spectrum is continuous; there is no reason for dividing it this way. In fact, the spectrum is not divided the same way in all languages. Speakers of Shona and Bassa in Africa, for example, divide it differently, as depicted below (Gleason, cited in Crane and Angrosino 1992:124).

ENGLISH	purple	blue	green	yellow	orange	red
SHONA	cips^wuka	citema	cicena		cips^wuka	
BASSA		hui		ziza		

Thus, humans do not categorize the color spectrum into distinct colors in the same way across the world. The Bassa use one word *hui* for the colors that we would call purple, blue, and green in English. The Bassa do not recognize contrasts between purple and blue or blue and green in their language as English speakers do. This does not mean that either the Bassa or the English system is better; they are just different. It is useful to understand how people categorize things and how they perceive similarity and contrast. The categories they devise have meaning for them, and the meaning of the category in which they place a thing affects the way they act toward that thing. In organizations, people categorize other workers, kinds of work, superiors, and so on. The process by which the anthropologist learns of these categories can be found in the work of James Spradley (1980), Nancy Morey and Fred Luthans (1984), and others.

The following is an example of the use of this process in an organizational assessment from which I learned how a CEO categorized employees. Notice that I did not ask the CEO to categorize employees. The information resulted from an open-ended question about organization history.

Q: Tell me about the history of the organization.

A: Well, originally it was a family-owned, family-controlled business. There was a caste system. The officers were the haves and the others were the have-nots. You could always tell the officers because they had alligator shoes on. There was lots of frustration, lots of drinking, and lots of chasing. Most of them didn't graduate from college. It was the "good ol' southern boy" type situation. Then in the sixties they began to bring in a few professional types who learned their stuff at other companies. Jones was brought in to run it. He hired good high-priced professional people from Zeta corporation. He demeaned the old people here and thought only the people he brought in were good. He screwed up the whole system. He brought in a guy to work under me and paid him the same as me, and this guy rode in the front of the airplane while I rode in the back. He told our clients the old people were not good. Well, he was fired about 15 years ago, and the company began to look for a buyer. The company was sold, and I became the head of it. There were all these different kinds of people. I called everyone in a room and said, "I don't care where you came from. I decide about you according to your performance." Jones left a hell of a legacy—more good people than we needed, so I cut back. Those Zeta people brought in training methods. They hired college people, college of business students who want to work hard and learn. We have some MBAs around here. I've worked with lots of MBAs who frustrate me. MBAs have such upward mobility expectations that they don't learn their job well enough to train the people behind them. I believe in internal training. That's what we learned from Zeta. That prepares people better than MBAs.

MY ANALYSIS

> *Domain:* Employees
>
> *Cultural Categories:*
>
> 1. **Nonprofessional people**—original employees, good ol' southern boys
>
>   **1.1** Officers—haves, alligator shoes, lots of frustration, lots of drinking, lots of chasing
>
>   **1.2** Others—have-nots
>
> 2. **Professional types**
>
>   **2.1** Professional training on the job
>
>   > **2.11** 1960s professional types—Jones, for example
>   >
>   > **2.12** Zeta people—were high-priced, brought in training methods

2.2 Professional training through education

    2.21 College people—want to work hard, want to learn, have undergraduate degrees

    2.22 MBAs—are frustrating, do not learn their jobs, are focused on moving up, do not train people behind them well

In essence, what is presented here is what an anthropologist would call a *native taxonomy*. This is a description of how the interviewee divides up some cultural domain. In this case the domain is types of employees. I would not assume, based on analysis of this passage alone, that I knew what the CEO was thinking—that I knew that he categorized employees according to this system or he acted on these categorizations. This analysis provides a possible clue, but it is necessary to conduct a further investigation to determine if these categories are actually important to the CEO and important in the way he behaves toward employees. In this case I found that promotions and firings could be tied to these categories, suggesting to me that the categories did have validity (Walck and Jordan 1993).

Another use of the interview is described by Barbara Stern, Craig Thompson, and Eric Arnould in trying to grasp the consumer's view of a sales encounter. They used the *critical incident technique* interview, which is used in marketing analysis, to get interviewees to describe a specific encounter with a sales representative. To this technique they added the characteristics of a *phenomenological interview*, in which they asked the interviewee to describe what happened before and after the incident so that they could understand the place the incident held in that interviewee's life. Understanding the context of the incident for the interviewee allows the researcher to know the interviewee's assessment of the incident. The interviewee is allowed to tell the story as he sees it. The researcher then analyzes the resulting narrative.

Stern, Thompson, and Arnould (1998:199) asked the interviewee to respond to the question: "Can you think of a shopping experience that you would like to talk about?" Their interviewee, Paul, described his experience when he went to a sporting goods store to buy a new pair of tennis shoes for aerobic exercise. In the course of the experience, Paul switched brands; he entered the store intent on buying Reeboks and left having bought Avias. Paul switched brands because he felt the Avia shoe was specifically designed for aerobics, his sport, and the Reebok was a multipurpose shoe. He became angry over the salesperson's attempt to get him to make a decision on price alone instead of on the shoe features, the important factor for Paul. In the course of their analysis, Stern et al. demonstrate the importance of the consumer's emotions in marketing relationships. The consumer responds to nurturing and empathy and a sense of fulfillment.

Another interview technique used by anthropologists studying consumer behavior is what Christina Wasson calls *store interrupt interviews,* in which a researcher video records a shopper's behavior and interrupts the shopper to ask questions about the purchase (Wasson 2000:383). In this technique, the researcher is able to learn the shopper's thoughts at the exact time of the recorded behavior. This gives the researcher valuable data in analyzing shopping behavior.

ANALYSIS OF EVENTS

In some cases, anthropologists find that certain features of an organization's life provide a window through which to view that life. While a researcher uses a variety of anthropological techniques to gain data about the organization, sometimes a focus on specific features is especially helpful.

In the course of participant observation in a community mental health center in the Midwestern United States, Helen Schwartzman (1989) and her research colleagues realized that as participants in the organization, they were attending many meetings, and the meetings were a vital clue to understanding the organization, which they named "Midwest." Schwartzman discovered that staff members had different roles in the organization than board members and that the staff and the board were caught up in a battle for control. Each group viewed the actions of the other as evidence that the other was "out of control." This could be best understood, Schwartzman felt, by attending and observing what took place in their meetings.

Staff and board respectively held their own meetings, and in their respective meetings the attendees described and interpreted events. Schwartzman found that in these meetings the two groups were describing different versions and interpretations of the same events. Thus, both groups were experiencing and generating a differing set of interpretations regarding the realities they all faced. The process and interaction of the meetings was an arena of social activity, which revealed the dynamics of this organization.

Schwartzman and her colleagues were using multiple research methods to understand "Midwest." They entered the center as researchers and did not participate in the staff functions. They observed behavior in the center and wrote these observations up as field notes. They observed and taped meetings, and they conducted interviews with the staff and board members that included questions about the observed meetings.

Other anthropologists have found that studying organizational events alone can provide valuable information about an organization. However, this approach does not have the same depth or breadth as a more thorough approach. Mary Jo Schneider gives us an analysis of Walmart that she gleaned from attending the annual shareholders' meeting for 20 years (Schneider 1998). In 1997, the final year of her study, over 17,000 shareholders, associates (the term Sam Walton used to refer to his workers), and analysts attended the annual meeting.

Eighty percent of those attending in 1997 were associates, and the shareholders' meeting was actually an extravagant display of Walmart culture intended for the benefit of the associates who arrived from around the country on chartered buses. The event included songs, cheers, appearances by nationally known entertainers, pep talks and company information from the company's executives, as well as recognition of outstanding performances and stories that illustrated the values Walmart wanted its associates to embody. The meeting was a good time for all participants. The presentations were delivered in a style that harkened back to the small-town Arkansas roots of the founder, Sam Walton.

Through analysis of the form and content of these shareholder meetings, Schneider demonstrated how the Walmart organization created an image of its stores as a return to the values and the ways of the "good old days" in small-town America, an image of Walmart as a patriotic good neighbor with integrity and openness that upholds traditional rural American values.

While purposely creating this image of itself, the reality was that Walmart was a modern multinational business. It satisfied its small-town customers by providing them with a variety of merchandise at reasonable prices; to do this, the organization was an active participant in the global economy. Products in the stores frequently came from foreign manufacturers or from foreign plants of US or Canadian manufacturers. The use of global manufacturing allowed Walmart to bring the customer a variety of goods at competitive prices. This tactic made Walmart, when measured in sales, the fourth largest company in the United States and the twelfth largest in the world.

Schneider's analysis provides an understanding of Walmart's two-pronged management strategy as it attempts to direct the "down home" organizational culture its retail workers accept while at the same time putting together an organization that participates in the global market as one of the largest international retailers. As of July 2012, its sales thus far for that year were $444 billion (http://investors.walmartstores.com/phoenix.zhtml?c=112761&p=irol-irhome).

ANALYSIS OF RELATIONSHIPS

Studying relationships provides another specific lens through which to analyze human behavior. In anthropology we have gathered much data in societies that have no formal legal systems; social relationships hold those societies together. Thus, we appreciate the importance of understanding social relationships in order to understand human behavior. Anthropologists were some of the first social scientists to focus on systematic social networks when they focused on kinship. Louis Henry Morgan's nineteenth-century kinship drawings were an early network maps of relations. W. Lloyd Warner, in his work at the Western Electric's Hawthorne Works described in chapter 2, was interested in the patterning of informal ties among the workers, and he systematically gathered data on interpersonal interaction. This resulted in social network data and graphic depictions of network ties (Gluesing 2013).

A network is a pattern of complex linkages between people. Some networks are formal, some are not. Anthropologists conduct *network analysis* to discover a structure or pattern in social situations where it is informal or hidden or where an old, formalized structure is undergoing such a great change that it no longer provides a functional skeleton for social interaction. In an organizational context, the formalized structure is represented by the organization chart. When repetitive interactions between individuals and groups are not recognized on organization charts, these charts can mislead us as we try to explain or make sense of organizational behaviors. The task of network analysis is to construct the pattern of linkages, reflected in the interactions and relationships between individuals and groups, to explain the behaviors in the organization.

From the broader perspective, however, the network is one piece of the larger puzzle, and the researcher is ultimately interested in how this network is integrated into the cultural whole of the organization. Thus, network analysis is used to understand with whom an individual or a group of individuals interacts *over a specified period of time*. In addition, the researcher is interested in some of the characteristics of the interactions, such as the circumstances under which the interactions occur, their purpose, the number of times they occur during the period studied, and so on. The specific characteristics anthropologists are interested in depend on the questions they are trying to answer in the study.

Today's anthropologists, however, have tools unavailable to Morgan or Warner in that we have computers and sophisticated software packages that allow easier analysis and visual display of elaborate, large networks. Brandon Ofem, Theresa Floyd, and Stephen Borgatti (2013) explain that the method works best in what they call an *ethnographic sandwich*. One begins with ethnographic data collection to learn about the organization, what possible networks are significant to one's research question, and how to phrase questions that will reveal these networks. Should you ask who each individual interacts with to get work done, or who each individual seeks advice from, or who they talk to during the day? How one frames the questions is determined by what kinds of relationships one is researching. This is the first slice of the ethnographic sandwich. Then the meat of the sandwich, the actual network data, is acquired by sending out a survey to all appropriate individuals. That data can then be visualized by putting it into network software such as NETDRAW in the UCINET network analysis package (Borgatti, Everett, and Freeman 2002). The final slice of the sandwich is to return to ethnography by showing the resulting network diagrams to the individuals surveyed and recording their reactions to gain richer insight into the network.

Calvin Morrill used network analysis in understanding conflict management among corporate executives (Morrill 1991). He worked with executives, defined as individuals holding at least the title of partner or vice president, in two companies. He gained access through personal ties with a consultant who worked with both companies. He explained his interest as that of an observer who wanted to learn about business. He spent 217 hours in one company and 236 hours in the other over a 14-month period. Of the two companies, one was an international accounting firm with over 20,000 employees, several dozen branch offices, and over $1 billion in sales. The other was a manufacturer of electronic learning aids, computers, and toys for children. It had 35,000 employees and over $1 billion in sales. Both companies were alike in that they were located in the same geographical area, were financially solvent, and had an executive force consisting primarily of white males between 35 and 60 years of age. They differed in that the manufacturer of toys was an international headquarters and the accounting firm was a regional headquarters, although it operated autonomously from the national headquarters.

Other differences were important. The accounting firm was owned by several hundred partners scattered over its branch offices. While the organization had a formal hierarchy, each partner had a great deal of autonomy, and most had been active in more than one branch office. At the toy manufacturer, the executives were organized so that departments—sales, finance, engineering, and so on—were crosscut by product teams, which were responsible for specific product lines. Each executive was likely to report to two bosses, one in his functional department and a second one in a product team.

In addition to gathering a good bit of descriptive data about activities in the two companies, Morrill conducted a network analysis. To do this, he asked executives in each company to identify the other executives in the company (1) to whom they regularly talked about work-related issues only, (2) from whom they regularly needed to receive information in order to make decisions, (3) on whom they had called in the last six months to be an ally during interpersonal problems or conflicts with other executives, and (4) with whom they regularly discussed interpersonal or other work-related problems. Morrill used additional interviewing (both formal and informal), observation in the companies (including shadowing an individual throughout the day and taking notes on his activities), and document collection to further understand how these executives viewed conflict management.

He found that partners in loosely knit organizational networks managed conflict without confrontation, while those in densely knit networks regularly confronted others with grievances. In the accounting firm, partners were relatively autonomous and socially distant, and conflict was handled "with little fanfare." In the toy manufacturer, executives were in close contact with and dependent on each other to form alliances for their points of view. Grievances here were confronted more directly. Beyond understanding the different conflict management practices of these two specific companies, Morrill contributed to our understanding of conflict management in complex organizations by demonstrating that organization structure and network density are important factors in conflict resolution.

Barbara Olsen conducted a marketing project that relied on a staple of traditional anthropology: *kinship analysis*. She wanted to know about the "cultural biography of brands and brand loyalty" (Olsen 1995:245). Brands that have the benefit of a strong following, such as Nike and Coca-Cola, use that benefit to further advantage themselves in the marketplace. Many companies go to great lengths to achieve brand recognition. Olsen was interested in the relationship between kinship, an area of culture long considered important by anthropologists, and brand loyalty. Through participant observation and interviews, she collected life-history material about shopping patterns and experience with brands.

Olsen found that brands may have a "nostalgia" equity and that kinship ties can produce strong brand loyalty. For example, one elderly Mexican woman explained that she always used Palmolive soap because her mother had used it and the smell of it always reminded her of her mother. A young Filipino man stated that in buying items for his own home, he "automatically" purchased Whirlpool for his kitchen; RCA for his TV; and Colgate, Listerine, and Ivory for his personal needs because these were the brands his family had always used. An Italian American woman in her 20s explained that she and her three sisters all used Gold Medal flour, Morton salt, Arm & Hammer baking soda, and Domino sugar because their mother and grandmother did also.

Olsen's work suggests the unusual possibility that looking at kinship ties, a traditional component of anthropological studies, may be important in understanding consumer behavior. Marketers have found that brand loyalty is waning as other factors like convenience, image of modernity, and cost become more important. Olsen shows that lineage consumption patterns continue to play a factor, however, giving established brand names equity. While Olsen used her traditional anthropological interest in kinship to explore a specific aspect of marketing relationships, marketers have long been interested in managing consumer–brand relationships in general.

SEMIOTIC ANALYSIS

Jean-Marie Floch demonstrated the usefulness of applying a *semiotic analysis* to product design, product packaging, and advertising. Her work is based on the work of French anthropologist Claude Lévi-Strauss who suggested that all human brains process information in the same way, regardless of cultural differences. All humans classify phenomena in terms of binary opposition so that, for example, female contrasts with male, light with dark, presence of a chair with absence of a chair, and so forth. Humans tangle these classifications together in complex ways that the researcher can untangle into the basic binary opposites.

Floch demonstrates how a rigorous semiotic analysis of logos, advertisements, and products can provide insight about how consumers relate to products. For example, she compares the logos of IBM and Apple and demonstrates how the Apple logo is in many ways a reaction to the IBM logo. The IBM logo of striped, blue, block letters gives the impression of speed and efficiency. Apple's logo, devised under the direction of the late Steve Jobs, actually makes a statement that Apple is not IBM. The Apple logo, the rainbow-colored apple with a bite out of it, references its rival in that it is also a strong, simple logo with lines through it. Further, it references the biblical story of Adam and Eve and the tree of knowledge. Its multicolored rainbow shades emphasize the warm colors of red, yellow, and orange in contrast to IBM's cold color of blue. The colors suggest the psychedelic age, and the apple suggests the vegetarian diet of the countercultural times of which Jobs was a product.

Floch uses this example to point out that a logo does not exist in isolation but exists instead in a context that gives it meaning. Floch demonstrates in her study of these logos that semiotic analysis is useful in understanding and developing advertising and product designs (Floch 2000).

VIDEO-BASED INTERACTION ANALYSIS

Interaction analysis is a method used to study how humans interact with each other and with objects in their environment. This method allows the anthropologist to look at talk, nonverbal interaction, and the use of artifacts and technologies. Whether one is observing activity in an airline operations room, at a manufacturing plant's planning meeting, in a classroom, during a medical consultation, or some other organizational setting, the activity is so multifaceted and complex it is impossible to record all of it accurately in field notes. At the Palo Alto Research Center and the Institute for Research on Learning, anthropologists found that videotaping interactions to augment traditional ethnographic techniques was invaluable for studying work and learning processes (Jordan and Henderson 1995).

The analysis of the videotapes is a collaborative venture by a group of researchers so that more than one opinion of the action is recorded and is likely to begin with identifying "ethnographic chunks" on the video. This means dividing the work seen on the video into smaller units of coherent action. In a medical consultation there might be a "medical history-taking" chunk and an "advice-giving" chunk, for example. Events usually have beginnings and endings that may be evident in the behavior on the video. In a meeting, moving from one topic to the next on the agenda may be accompanied by the activities of closing the folder containing the information on the former topic and opening the folder containing the information on the next topic. In the operations room at an airline hub, the transition from a slow period to a busy period may be marked by the operators squaring themselves in their chairs and changing the tone of their conversation. The actions on the video allow researchers to determine "chunks" of activity, which is helpful in understanding the ways in which time is organized in the moment-to-moment, real-time interaction in a situation.

Using video-based interaction analysis, anthropologists learn what is conducive to on-the-job learning. Videos allow the anthropologists to capture the rhythm of work activity. Their analysis suggests that certain kinds of rhythms in the workplace allow for more learning by new workers. If the work is performed at a steady pace and requires the full attention of the worker, a trainee is likely to learn less than if the rhythm of the work includes a regular "downtime," or slack period. It is during the slack period that the trainee can ask questions and clarify points. This is the time the trainee clarifies what has happened and learns what is expected next. Trainees learn faster when the work has a rhythm that includes these "downtimes."

The video reveals the behavior of turn taking. Individuals engaged in conversation engage in turn taking in their talk, but turn taking in many work contexts includes taking turns at physical activities as well. For example, it is important to understand what patterns of turn taking and collaborative behavior in manipulating objects are conducive to learning and a smooth work process. When workers are problem solving they interact differently when all are using a single computer than when each has access to her own computer. These differences can impact learning and the smooth progression of the work process.

The video also captures the spatial relationships in the room and the relationships among the humans and between humans and machines. Individuals often make statements through the way in which they occupy space. At a meeting involving two work groups, the leader of one signaled her dominance by occupying the chair at the head of the long, rectangular table, while the leader of the other signaled a subordinated status by occupying a seat along the wall, avoiding the table all together. In this research the anthropologists can learn how use of the spatial environment encourages or hinders interaction among workers. Objects are frequently used as territorial markers. These markers can be seen in the way one decorates one's office or cubical or in the way one arranges one's coffee cup, papers, and pen so as to mark off his space when sitting at a table with other participants in a meeting. The arrangement of the space can assist the successful completion of work or get in the way of it. Video analysis helps researchers understand what the best configuration is for the space, whether that be locations of desks, locations of computers, or configurations of computers.

Some artifacts and documents are owned by some individuals in an interaction and not others. In a medical consultation, the doctor looks at the chart and converses with the patient; she does not offer the chart to the patient as a shared document for him to survey. She signals her ownership of this important artifact. Understanding how artifacts are owned and/or controlled in the workplace can have important implications for success and efficiency of the work process. It can also help the employer create learning environments for new members of the work team. Anthropologists have found interaction analysis to be a powerful tool in the investigation of human activity, particularly effective in complex, multi-actor, technology-mediated work settings and learning environments.

In fact, in the study of product design, anthropologists realized that a picture can be worth a thousand words. Christina Wasson (2000:382–383) describes her work for E-Lab where on one occasion she used eight mounted cameras in various parts of an office and on another occasion she used seven cameras in a store. She left the cameras running throughout business hours, in order to capture the human behavior. She also used roving cameras, where a researcher using a handheld camera asked a worker to describe everything in her work environment or where a researcher followed a shopper, recording his every behavior.

In the office project she was interested in how workers interact with their physical environment and with objects in that environment in order for her client to design office environments that would better support the changing nature of work. In the store project she was interested in shoppers' behavior, especially their process of product selection and decision making. In the office project she learned about worker behavior, unmet needs, and the history of social arrangements. In the store project, which also included in-depth interviews in shoppers' homes, she learned about the histories, experiences, needs, and values that shaped the shopping behavior of the shoppers and their families.

A related technique anthropologists also use is to give their subjects disposable cameras and ask them to take pictures documenting their behavior in the context under investigation and to provide a written description of the meaning of the pictures.

VIRTUAL ETHNOGRAPHY AND MAKING USE OF ELECTRONIC DATA

In today's world of multinational corporations, global partnerships, and complex relationships, social network analysis is useful for understanding global organizing, how to manage a team of workers who are not colocated but rather scattered all around the world. A wealth of valuable electronic data are available to anthropologists through the Internet. This includes corporate websites, e-mails, and social networking sites. Methods are being developed to capture this data for use in ethnography.

For example, Julia Gluesing and her colleagues (2013) devised a method for mining company e-mails to better understand global organizing in a multinational corporation. Specifically they studied the employees in an automobile company who were involved in developing new, hands-free technologies to be installed in models of the cars the company manufactured. Gluesing studied all work teams and divisions involved in developing the products, including members of the core product team, members of the design and ergonomics team, and people who worked in the Office of the General Council. The hands-free technologies would have to be "sold" to people who worked in other divisions of the company, and they would have the choice of whether to incorporate the new products in future car models. Managers wanted to know how successfully these new products were being received by those who would ultimately make decisions about their adoption. Was the "buzz" in the company loud, extensive, and positive?

Gluesing and the others employed a mixed-method approach to learn about how this innovation was being received. They recruited participants for their study and, with the participants' permission, captured their e-mails about the new, hands-free products. Since the participants were located all over the world, this technique was an efficient way to collect data. E-mails were studied for network data—that is, who e-mails whom and about what? They were also studied for content; in these e-mails, were the employees making positive or enthusiastic statements about the new products? Thirty-eight people participated in the study resulting in 45,000 e-mails and links to over 2,000 people across the enterprise. Quantitative techniques were used for this analysis.

In addition to gathering e-mail data, the researchers used interviewing and shadowing to get a richer understanding of the data provided by the e-mail analysis. Reminiscent of the ethnographic sandwich, the ethnographic data provided details unavailable from the computer-gathered data. For example, the e-mails did not capture discussions in the hallways and face-to-face meetings. Nor did they reveal cultural differences, such as managers in the primary European location did not use e-mail to communicate with others whose offices were close by but instead preferred to communicate with them in person. As a result, the research team was able to develop a set of computer tools for managers to use to gauge the level of receptiveness to any innovative design. Network analysis using e-mail and other digital media will become more commonplace in conducting multisited ethnography in global organizations.

Virtual ethnographic techniques are important in consumer research. Jennifer Cardew Kersey (2009) explains that Web research might focus on a: (1) virtual space, (2) a group of people across many websites, or (3) a topic across many websites and groups. Data gathering involves nontext artifacts such as videos, emoticons, and avatars. Online research means mining the Web for artifacts that relate to the client's research questions. The researcher then captures the Web content using one of the online clipping services that allows for text, video, screen shots, and images to be captured and catalogued. Much of this material may be subsequently downloaded into a coding software, such as ATLAS.ti, and further analyzed.

The researcher also keeps a journal of all his "travels" through the Web in search of artifacts. The deliverables to the client are likely to include an archive of all the digital artifacts captured, a map of search engine pathways, and a list of important websites containing consumer reactions to the client's products. Cardew Kersey thinks online data are most useful when balanced with offline data, because in some cases the two disagree and one without the other can be misleading. For example, people might complain heartily about a product when they contribute to an online blog but are less negative when directly interviewed. Of course our anthropological skills of recognizing an important artifact, seeing patterns in behavior, and thinking holistically are just as important in the virtual world as in the real one, and results for the client ultimately depend on these skills of data interpretation. In the future, research in the virtual world can only become more significant.

It is important to realize, however, there are new ethical issues for anthropologists working in virtual field sites. The Web makes it easy for all of us to appear as someone we are not, and data should not be drawn from private sites unless one's researcher status is announced.

MULTIPLE TECHNIQUES AND RAPID ASSESSMENT

In business anthropology, it is frequently necessary to conduct fieldwork over a relatively short period of time—a few days, weeks, or months. (Traditionally, anthropological fieldwork was conducted for a one-year period.) To do so and gain accurate information, business anthropologists use several techniques in any specific project. The majority of anthropologists combine observation, interviewing, and the collection of artifacts and documents as techniques appropriate to almost all data gathering. They may add other techniques as the situation warrants. This kind of multiple-technique approach is common in most anthropological assessments.

Frequently researchers check their results through triangulation. According to James Beebe (2000:30–33), triangulation is a term originally used in navigation and physical surveying but has been borrowed by social scientists to represent a way of validating data by reaching the same conclusion through at least two pieces of data. In social science, triangulation can be achieved by using data from different sources, using several different researchers to gather and evaluate the data, using multiple theoretical perspectives to analyze the data, and/ or using multiple methods to study the problem.

Beebe advocates using teams as a form of triangulation to gather data when conducting a rapid assessment. The team is likely to gain more reliable data than a single researcher. Team members should come from different perspectives. For example, in interviewing the director of a nonprofit organization, a three-member team might include a human relations/personnel specialist, a financial specialist, as well as a lead researcher who will initiate the interview questions. All three ask questions, however. The financial specialist might ask about the recent failure to complete a scheduled audit, while the human relations expert might be interested in recent personnel policy changes. The variety of their questions allows for richer interview data to emerge and assures that more than one point of view will be expressed through the interview questions. This is a form of triangulation. Did the researchers see the same changes? Did the findings from one technique support the findings from another? In a rapid assessment, we are careful not to lose accuracy (Beebe 2000).

CONCLUSION

This chapter is only an introduction to anthropological field techniques; anthropologists use many techniques I have not mentioned here. The techniques I selected are suited for a variety of different purposes. For example, if one wanted to conduct a broad survey of shopping mall behavior, one might roam the mall with video cameras and conduct shopping interrupt interviews. Lengthy and detailed interviews designed to elicit native taxonomy would not be appropriate in this circumstance as they would provide more detail and less breadth than the research requires. Conversely, if one were trying to understand the behaviors, perceptions, and work and decision-making processes of a self-managed work team, one might conduct lengthy interviews, some loosely structured and others more specific, and observe the team for weeks or months. This fine-grained approach provides depth and subtle details that allow one to analyze the processes the team uses to function. It provides more data about a small number of subjects.

Which methods researchers choose would depend on the research questions they are seeking to answer as well as their available resources. Anthropologists tailor their use of techniques to the purpose of the research and to the resources available to conduct the study. With a wide variety of techniques in our tool bag, we are able to pick and choose the ones most appropriate for each project.

While anthropologists are specialists in qualitative methods, they appreciate the value of quantitative methods as well and frequently incorporate them into their work, just as Gluesing did in her study of global organizing in an automobile company. Qualitative methods used in conjunction with quantitative ones tap the subtexts or additional information not always evident from the quantitative data. Our goal, after all, is to understand human behavior. Gathering data in multiple ways increases the likelihood of getting a well-rounded picture of human life so that researchers can better understand the issues that impact the problem they are addressing.

Anthropologist and consumer-behavior researcher Daniel Miller explained that ethnography is more than a method: it reflects a commitment—a commitment to the people being studied, not just the objects; a commitment to understanding what people actually do, not just what they say they do; a commitment to study people in the context of their regular lives, not just a circumstance created by the researchers; and a commitment to understand people within the larger context of their lives (holism), not just in the context of the transaction under study (Miller 1997:16–17).

Chapter Four

Seeing
Cultural Groupings

What anthropologists have to offer . . .

"I remember a fire in the Bronx. . . . It was the 4th of July. . . . What happened is that a rocket went through an open window in the [apartment] building and started a fire in the rear. . . . When we got to the 8th floor, we saw smoke. Smoke was filling the apartment, real black stuff, plastic yuck. . . . So we forced the door. . . . The smoke just blew out the door, flooded the hallway, and went down 8 floors into the lobby. . . . Then a guy [firefighter] . . . on the floor above us started yelling, "The fire's now in the room next to you! You gotta get out of there!" . . . [The other firefighter in the room with me] had taken out the window. The roof man dropped down a rope to us and held it. And we slid under our own power down to the 7th floor." (Kaprow 1999:7)

This narrative, collected by anthropologist Miriam Kaprow from a New York City firefighter, demonstrates the ethnographic method of gathering information about workers (firefighters) doing their job. What makes this approach different from that of other organizational behavior specialists and consumer-behavior analysts?

The need to study human behavior in natural settings led to the development of the ethnographic method of anthropology (which is discussed in chapter 3). It also led to the development of the *culture construct* as an effective means to collect and organize the data. The culture construct provides a means of identifying the set of behaviors unique to each human group and distinguishing it from the behavior of others.

Just what is it about the anthropological approach that is unique and valuable? There is no simple answer to that question as the anthropological approach can take one of multiple directions whether one is analyzing organizations, designing new products, or developing marketing strategies. However, in order to make it easier to conceptualize how an anthropologist works in business, this chapter discusses the construct, "culture," one of the markers of our approach that a business anthropologist might use.

USING THE ANTHROPOLOGICAL CONSTRUCT OF CULTURE TO UNDERSTAND HUMAN BEHAVIOR

The number of anthropological definitions of culture are legion, and consequently the single definition of culture used here is not universally accepted by anthropologists.[1] Some anthropologists prefer a mentalist definition of culture, which states that culture is in one's head; it is the set of rules that one has learned that then determine one's actions. Others prefer omnibus definitions that state that culture is not only the knowledge one carries in one's head but also the behavior that results and the artifacts (material objects) that are created to use with those behaviors (McCurdy et al. 2005). In working in business, I prefer an omnibus definition. It foregrounds behavior and artifacts as well as knowledge and makes clear that all three must be considered in order to understand culture. So I will define culture here as an integrated system of shared ideas (thoughts, ideals, attitudes), behaviors (actions), and material artifacts (objects) that characterize a group (adapted from Heibert, 1976:25).

When this concept was developed in anthropology, the developers envisioned cultures as isolated wholes in which all features of cultural life were interrelated and integrated. In studying the Trobriand islanders, for example, early anthropologists like Malinowski could envision Trobriand culture with clear boundaries. One was either a Trobriander and a participant in Trobriand culture, or one was not. The Trobrianders were a culturally isolated group just as they were a geographically isolated one since they lived on islands surrounded by the Pacific Ocean. Today, anthropologists know that this monolithic notion of culture makes no real sense. No cultural group is an island, isolated from the influences of others. Culture is much messier, more complex, and, frankly, more interesting than that.

The world is now experiencing what may be the greatest migration of peoples in all of human history. War, famine, and the economic opportunities of a global market are some of the causes. New geographic groupings are developing: in Asia the grouping of Taiwan,

Hong Kong, and Guangshou and in North America the grouping of
Mexico, California, Texas, and Arizona are examples of new economically and culturally linked areas that crosscut old cultural boundaries
and current state systems (Costa and Bamossy 1995:3–4).

Over the years, anthropologists have changed their preconceptions to align with a more accurate understanding of the world. Richard
Wilk provides a good example of this in his 1991 book about the Kekchi
Maya in Belize. He explains how his perspective changed between 1978
and 1991. In 1978, he envisioned the Kekchi as a traditional people
who were isolated from the outside world and resistant to the intrusion
of Western culture but who would ultimately be forced into the Western
economy in a way that would lead to the loss of their own traditional
culture. By 1991, Wilk realized that he had been viewing the Kekchi
through an outdated and inaccurate lens. In fact, the Kekchi had been
integrated into the world economy in a variety of ways for at least 400
years as they supplemented their horticultural subsistence strategies
with work off the farm and with exchange of goods and services with
outsiders. While he found it true that much of their interaction with the
world economy was in situations where they were economically dominated and exploited by others, he also found their cultural identity was
possibly strengthened rather than weakened by these experiences
(Wilk 1991:5–6).

Wilk's example of the Kekchi fits many of the indigenous cultural
groupings around the world, which anthropologists have depicted as
homogeneous, isolated, and doomed to loss due to modernization.
Anthropologists now realize that it is more useful to look at the ways in
which cultural groupings interact, realizing that the people on the
receiving end of Western culture have *agency*. They pick and choose
what works for them and how. As David Howes explains it, we are not
experiencing the "Coca-colonization" of the world, the view that goods
like Coca-Cola flow from the West to the rest of the world, causing the
homogenization of culture in the process. Instead we are experiencing
the "creolization" of the world in that goods flow back and forth around
the world and are adapted in new areas in proportion to their usefulness. In addition, the uses of those goods in new cultural environments
may be ones the original producers never envisioned.

Anthropologists now focus on modes of consumption as much as
they focus on modes of production. The consumption of a single product
around the world, Coca-Cola for example, is recontextualized in each
new environment. In fact, Coke has been used to reduce wrinkles in
Russia, bring people back to life in Haiti, and turn copper into silver in
Barbados (Howes 1996a:6). In another example, the Mendi of Papua
New Guinea have used safety pins for earrings, used umbrella spokes
for combs, and rolled bits of plastic bags into twine to use in making net
bags (Howes 1996a:5).

Also, in looking at our very mobile and complex world, obviously one cannot even pigeonhole people into one cultural identity. What exactly is African American culture or Anglo-American culture, for example? While culture still defines a coherent group or community, culture is not homogeneous and the boundaries of the cultural group are not clear. Instead, what anthropologists see as we look out across the cultural landscape is a complex web of interacting cultural groups and individual humans who fit into multiple cultural groups. Not only are the groups interacting, redefining cultural space, and contesting the behaviors and values of other groups, but individuals cannot easily be placed within single groups. The boundaries of the cultural groups are flexible, permeable, and not clearly defined (Marcus 1998:6). An individual may identify with one group at one moment and another group at the next moment or may identify with more than one group at the same time.

Consider ethnic identity for a moment. In the United States many people identify themselves with a single ethnic group—African American or Anglo-American, for example. What if an individual has one parent who is African American and one parent who is Anglo-American? Which group represents her ethnic identity? Perhaps one's parents immigrated to Canada as young adults, and one of them is of the Han ethnic group of China and the other is from Iran. The child of this union, however, was born in Canada and considers himself culturally, thoroughly "North American." Is he Chinese, Iranian, or North American? What about someone who is American Indian, and of his four grandparents, one was German, one was a full-blood Choctaw, and two were full-blood Cherokees? While this individual is three-fourths American Indian, is he a Choctaw or a Cherokee? What about the one-quarter German ancestry? To confuse matters more, what if this individual was adopted at birth by an Anglo-American family of Russian Jewish descent and was raised in the Russian Jewish tradition? He is American/Russian Jewish in cultural grouping, while his physical heritage is predominantly American Indian. In addition, all Americans of Russian Jewish background do not think and act alike, nor do all American Indians or all Cherokees. So what is this person's identity? Just as these examples demonstrate, identifying the members of any cultural grouping may be quite difficult.

One of the ways in which anthropologists contribute to understanding human life is by interpreting how humans are part of culture—a web of cultures, actually. Any individual living in this complex, postindustrial age is likely to identify with a number of cultural groupings that may have poorly defined and permeable boundaries. Furthermore, the groupings are typically overlapping and interconnected, contested and cooperative: a web of interaction in which actions add to future content. What a confusing picture! Anthropologists untangle this web by identifying the various cultural groupings and the interactions of individuals who can act at one moment as part of one cultural grouping and the next as part of another.

Frank Dubinskas, for example, unraveled the different notions of "time" as viewed by managers and scientists who worked in the biotechnology industry. The managers worked from a perspective of finite, economic realities—short-term planning and closed-frame problem solving; the scientists in the same organization worked from a model of the infinite expansion of scientific knowledge—open-ended planning and long-term problem solving. In situations where the two groups worked together for the same organizational goals, their diverse models of time caused friction that seemed insurmountable (Dubinskas 1988:11). Nevertheless, when operating in a different context, such as the role of parent, the behavior of those managers and scientists might be similar, if not identical, to each other. The construct of cultural groupings provides a way to unravel the complexity of interactions in this wild and crazy world of ours.

The *Shared* Characteristic of Culture

To explain the culture construct further, I want to discuss some characteristics of culture. Culture is found in *shared* patterns. For example, in trying to identify the culture of the Trobriand islanders, an anthropologist would watch for articulated ideas and behaviors shared by most members of the group. Most human behavior is cultural. Anthropologically, deviance from the culture is expected, identified, and its relationship to the group pattern understood; in fact, even deviance falls within a range that is culturally defined. Deviance takes two forms. The first of these is the individual behaviors not characteristic of the group pattern; these behaviors are idiosyncratic. The anthropologist identifies these behaviors and explains their relationship to the group pattern. The second form of cultural deviance is group behaviors that do not fit the pattern. Explaining the reasons for their existence and their relationship to the established patterns is the work of anthropology as well. Patterns not integrated into the cultural whole may indicate any number of different cultural issues. For example, it may indicate culture in the process of change, where some facets of the culture have changed and others have not. Or, the lack of integration may be due to the complexity of the interactions among overlapping and contested cultures.

So, why was Miriam Kaprow hanging out at the fire station collecting statements like the one that opened this chapter? While Kaprow studied firefighters prior to the World Trade Center disaster, what she learned can help us better understand the heroic behavior of firefighters on September 11, 2001. Kaprow learned that in New York City there was stiff competition for jobs as firefighters, even though the job is extremely hazardous. The fire academy accepted only 5 percent

of its applicants. After finishing at the academy, a prospective firefighter would still have to wait one to four years for a position. In addition, firefighters came to work early, stayed late, and brought their
families in on their days off. Many who were not disabled from the work
continued in the job ten years or more after the standard 20 years of
service. They donated money to fire-related charities (Kaprow
1999:107). Almost no New York City firefighters chose to transfer to the
police department, but the transfer rate from the police department to
the fire department was almost 30 percent, even though salaries and
mortality rates were equivalent.

Kaprow wanted to find out why firefighting was such a desirable
job and why firefighters were willing to go so far beyond the essentials
in doing their job. What she learned was that firefighting was a job that
had not been "proletarianized," meaning that firefighters had not lost
control of their work and had autonomy and control over the planning,
organization, and completion of their work. Their job had not been "deskilled" by being broken down into small chunks that could be performed by semiskilled or unskilled laborers. Being a police officer, by
contrast, was dangerous but less fulfilling, as a police officer did not
control the outcome of his work. Arrests made at personal peril were
overturned on technicalities, and police work was highly regulated by
the police department. Kaprow found that the ability to maintain control over a job requiring great skill provided the reward that made firefighting an enviable job to have and one for which it was worth working
overtime. As Chief Sean Flannery told her,

> "Next thing you know, you're looking forward to doing it. I don't
> know why, it's just kind of exciting. . . . You want to go to fires. . . .
> You wanted to go in, breathe smoke, break down doors, try to rescue
> people, cut roofs. . . . Afterwards you were spent, but it was a good
> feeling. It was hard work, but when it's out you saw the results of
> what you did. It was great. You're hot shit. . . . You loved to come to
> work and you loved to work hard. You wanted to go to fires. The
> whole atmosphere was great." (Kaprow 1999:10)

Kaprow identified the shared pattern of the professional culture of
firefighters. The culture centered on the heroic characteristics of the job,
the rituals like the communal dinner meal at the firehouse, and the code
of behavior and beliefs firefighters shared. Understanding this culture
allowed her to understand the appeal of the work. While other professional occupations, even medicine, law, and academia, have succumbed
to proletarianization, firefighting has not (Kaprow 1991, 1999).

The *Learned* Characteristic of Culture

Culture has several other characteristics that are important to
emphasize. Culture is *learned*; it is transmitted to new members

through a learning process. In one's primary culture, this process begins at birth. An infant is immediately subjected to culture in the form of the language she hears and the child-rearing practices to which she is submitted. When one joins an organization, one is immersed in a new culture, although it is a secondary one, not as significant as the primary culture learned at birth. Thus, in an organization the anthropologist can focus on the learning process. Training programs are, of course, one source of this learning, but other sources are the verbal asides of employees, the stories, ceremonies, myths, and especially the shared behavior patterns of employees.

In an example of professional culture that demonstrates its learned characteristic, Eileen Mulhare (1999) explains why in the professional culture of nonprofit management, strategic planning (a term that refers to a variety of management practices by which the company tries to align actions with goals) has remained an important tool in the manager's organization toolbox, even though management theorists and management behaviorists have been explaining since the 1970s that strategic planning does not produce better results than the less-organized, day-to-day, piecemeal approach to planning; additionally, strategic planning may even reduce creativity and innovation. Thus, it has fallen into disfavor in corporate settings.

What Mulhare learned was that the field of nonprofit management emerged as a profession in the 1980s when strategic management was popular. Universities across the country developed programs to train nonprofit managers. The first of these, the Program on Nonprofit Organizations, was created in 1976 at Yale University. By the mid-1990s, over 60 colleges and universities in North America offered programs. In the 1980s the popularity of nonquantitative strategic planning led to its becoming a common part of the "best practices" taught in these programs. It was during the 1980s that strategic planning so infiltrated the new profession of nonprofit management that most nonprofits assumed it to be part of best practices, and granting agencies required a strategic plan in grant applications. This enthusiasm for the technique continued in the 1990s even though business analysts became increasingly disenchanted with it and dropped it from their best practices.

Why has strategic planning remained a part of the nonprofit bible? Mulhare believes this is due to the professional culture that nonprofit managers learned. They were socialized or trained in management in programs that advocated the strategic planning approach. Thus, they were reluctant to abandon the approach because it had become an ideology. Even when confronted with cases where it clearly did not work, believers attributed the failure of the strategic plan to a failure in its execution and never questioned the validity of the technique itself. Anthropologists know this is a common reaction to failure of beliefs among members of a culture. Rather than question the belief, the execution of the belief is assumed to be faulty (Mulhare 1999:323–330). Anthropologists see that many professional groups exhibit patterns of group behavior; the members of the group have the same values and behave in similar ways. This is due to the similar training and similar required work behavior through which they learn to be part of this cultural grouping.

The *Symbolic* Characteristic of Culture

A symbol is any object or event that is used to represent or stand for another object or event. The meaning of a symbol is arbitrarily created by its users. Culture is a system of symbols, the meanings of which have been arbitrarily chosen by the culture bearers. Others cannot understand these meanings intuitively but must learn them. The process of enculturation is the process of teaching the young the symbols of their cultural system. A symbol is anything and everything that transmits culture, including language and jargon, myths and ceremonies, dress, furniture and spatial arrangements, all artifacts, and behavior patterns.

To learn a culture, one learns a symbol system. For example, not all cultures use the handshake as a form of greeting. It is a symbolic gesture understood by those familiar with cultures of the West but not understood universally. In one culture in South America, spitting on one another's chest is a form of greeting. Clearly the symbolic meaning of this gesture would need to be taught to Westerners in order to avoid their misinterpretation of the symbol because to spit on someone has a different and more hostile symbolic meaning in the cultures of the West. In organizations, the symbols include not only logos, slogans, and ceremonies but also the cultural symbols of behavior, such as a relaxed atmosphere where employees dress casually and exchange ideas in informal chats, or a more formal atmosphere with traditional business dress and all significant communication conducted in scheduled meetings with a set agenda. In either case, the attire and the behavior represent culture, a symbol system that one learns.

An example of greetings as a learned symbol system practiced in an organization is Lee Baker's 1995 study of ethnic difference in forms of address in the workplace. The traditional African American form of address used within structured settings such as church, office, or school is *title + name reciprocity*. This means that an individual would greet another by title and last name and the other individual would respond in the same manner. This telephone conversation is an example:

Staff 1: Hello, may I please speak with Mr. Foley?
Staff 1: It's Ms. Johnson.
Staff 1: Mr. Foley, it's Ms. Johnson in Admissions. I would like to
        know . . . (Baker 1995:191)

The general impetus for this form of address is respect and deference, not the demarcation of social hierarchies. When Euro-Americans use this pattern of title-and-name form of address, it is meant to mark special hierarchy. On the other hand, Euro-Americans frequently use *first name reciprocity* as the form of address in organizations. One reason for this is to give the impression of equality, even if a conversation is not between organizational equals. For example:

Manager: Billy, how's the monthly plan coming? We need it tomorrow.
Asst. Mgr.: Rick, you know I'll have it. (Baker 1995:190)

In both the African American and Euro-American cases, the speakers consider their form of address to be the most natural. They do not consider that in each case the difference is cultural and represents a difference in symbolic meaning between Euro-Americans and African Americans. Use of one's own cultural form of address with members of the other cultural grouping allows for misinterpretation, just as shaking hands or spitting on another's chest might. It is the role of the anthropologist as culture broker to explain these cultural differences and by doing so to prevent misunderstanding.

Annamma Joy, Michael Hui, Chankon Kim, and Michel Laroche's research on Italian immigrants in Montreal is an example of the symbolic nature of culture in a study of consumer behavior. Many of the immigrants they studied came from rural areas in Italy, where families raised animals, cultivated gardens, and purchased only a few food items like salt and cheese. Being accustomed to such a pattern in Italy, these immigrants felt it was important to live in their own homes and have gardens in Montreal. Joy and the others found that the Italians in Montreal who were sufficiently wealthy lived in single-family homes, while the less wealthy lived in triplexes, which had apartments to rent as well as a main house. In the yards of their homes, both the wealthy and less-wealthy immigrants planted gardens in which they grew tomatoes, parsley, corn, and other vegetables. Fruit was equally valued, and many had brought cuttings from plants or trees in their gardens in Italy to replant in their gardens at their new homes. Those who could afford it fashioned the look of their homes after Italian villas by constructing such features as columns, porticoes with archways, marble stairways, and geometric brickwork on the facade. To understand the consumer behavior of these immigrants, one must understand the symbolic importance of re-creating their Italian surroundings through their home purchases in this new land (Joy et al. 1995:145–179). They consume products that remind them of their Italian homeland rather than products that symbolically represent North America.

The *Adaptive* Characteristic of Culture

Culture can and does change, and it can and does change in relation to the environment; culture is *adaptive*. Any organization's culture must adapt to changes in its market environment to survive. This adaptive characteristic of culture represents a significant area of research. The theory used traditionally in anthropology to understand how groups of people adapt their culture to survival in a particular environment can be applied to business.

For example, in an agricultural society, people typically live permanently in one location. This allows them to watch their crops and stay near their stored crops after harvest. In contrast, people who get all their food by hunting wild animals and gathering wild plants typically move frequently as animals move and as different wild plants ripen. The settled agriculturalists have permanent homes while the mobile hunters and gatherers have dwellings that are easy to construct and to move. The dwelling type, mobility pattern, and subsistence strategy are all parts of culture. So a group typically has a culture that fits with its subsistence strategy. For a business organization, the organizational culture should be adaptive to the market environment in the same way an agriculturalist culture should be adaptive to its natural environment. A rigid, slowly changing culture is not a successful form of adaptation for a software development firm, for example, because such a firm requires a more flexible, fast-changing culture in order to respond to a rapidly changing market.

In studying consumer behavior, anthropologists often find examples of adaptation. Ayse Caglar described an interesting adaptive process in a study of fast food in Germany. Caglar reported in 1995 that there were 1.8 million Turkish immigrants in Germany and 35,000 Turkish-run businesses for a total Turkish business investment of 7.2 billion German marks. Eighty-seven percent of these businesses were in the restaurant field, with the large majority of them being fast-food stands. While the percentage of Turks in the food business in their home country was much smaller and their economic strategies there were much more varied, these immigrants found an economic niche they could fill in Germany. Their primary food product was the *doner kebap*, a sandwich of grilled meat with lettuce, tomato, cucumbers, red cabbage, onions, and a garlic yogurt or hot ketchup sauce.

The *doner kebap* so popular in Germany is not a fast food in Turkey, nor is it seasoned the same or served on the same type of bread. The bread most commonly used in Germany for the *doner kebap* is *pide* bread, which in Turkey is a special type of bread served only during the holy month of Ramadan. In Germany, where *pide* is served daily with the *doner kebap*, the Turkish immigrants used a different, special type of *pide* bread to serve only during their celebration of Ramadan. Thus, the Turks in Germany adapted their cultural pattern to the new situation: they continued to serve a special bread during Ramadan, which was not served other times of the year, while the bread eaten only during Ramadan in Turkey was being eaten daily in Germany.

Turkish vendors adapted other cultural patterns as well. Some food stand owners have given their stands names like McDoner or McKebap to make use of the successful McDonald's image. As one stand owner explained, "You know, here in Germany, everything American has a better value . . . there is this phenomena of McDonald's. I think they wanted to imitate it [McDonald's]" (Caglar 1995:220). Whether the German market was lacking in fast foods or whether the Turks were simply able to market a new fast-food taste successfully, the immigrants were able to establish themselves in this economically lucrative niche. This was an adaptive strategy employed by the Turks in Germany.

CULTURAL GROUPINGS IN ORGANIZATIONS

What does Allen Batteau (2000; 2001; 2010) mean when he suggests that there is a "safety culture" in the aviation industry? He is referring to a commitment to safety that affects decision making in both the organizational environment of the multinational aviation industry and the individual cockpit. "Safety culture" includes attention to detail, carefully following procedures, open communication, and never trading safety for a chance to make more money. In studying aviation safety culture, Batteau is studying organizational culture.

In this chapter, I have used several examples of anthropologists applying their understanding of cultural groupings to understanding organizations. These examples include Kaprow's work on the professional culture of firefighters, Baker's study of ethnic forms of address in the workplace, and Dubinskas' analysis of different notions of time among managers and scientists in a biotechnology firm. This anthropological understanding of cultural groupings in organizations is a unique contribution of our work to the field of organizational research. In order to understand why this is so, I contrast the anthropological approach to that of other organizational behavior specialists whose research training is based in psychology and sociology. While many of these organizational specialists now use the term *culture* in their analysis of organizations (since the publication of Deal and Kennedy's book, *Corporate Cultures* in the 1980s, the term has become common in organization studies), they use the term differently from how anthropologists use it.

The traditional organization studies' paradigm comes from psychology and views an organization as having three levels of structure: the individual, the group, and the organization. This view is depicted in figure 1. At the individual or micro level, it focuses on individual behavior with extensive understanding of individual motivation and

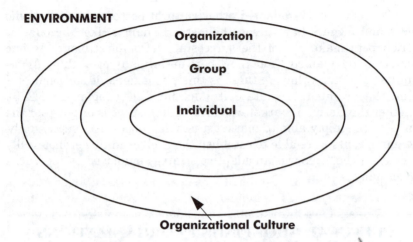

Figure 1 Organizational Behavior Perspective on Culture and Organization: Three Levels for Analyzing Organizational Events

personality and the necessity of developing jobs and reward systems that will motivate individuals to behave as the employer wishes. Thus, at the micro level, organization studies draws primarily on psychological theory. At the group level, the focus is on managing relationships among individuals, and the research focuses on group formation, structure, norms, and conflict. When researching the organization as a whole, one jumps to a macro level, where the individual's behavior falls from view. Here one is interested in the creation of an organization in which purpose, structure, and technology all function efficiently with the external environment. Leaders are the catalysts responsible for constructing this fit. In addition to structure, processes like communication, decision making, and change are also analyzed. At the group and macro levels, organization studies draw primarily on sociological and economic theories.

Culture, from the organization studies' perspective, represents one of the characteristics of an organization at the organization level, or macro level, of analysis. This characteristic is the "unwritten feeling" (Cherrington, 1989:498) part of the organization and usually represents values, beliefs, and shared understanding. It is considered to be intangible and difficult to define and measure. Harrison Trice and Janice Beyer (1993:5) suggest that the cultural approach as used in organization studies is most useful when it helps to explain neglected or overlooked aspects of organizations and when the concepts of other approaches are integrated with it. From this perspective, culture addresses aspects of organizations that are neglected in other organizational research. This accounts for the endurance of the concept of culture that began as a business buzzword and fad in the 1980s.

As an anthropologist, I look at a business organization and view organizational culture differently than someone trained in organizational behavior. Recall the definition of culture that I discussed at the beginning of the chapter: a culture is an integrated system of shared ideas, behaviors, and artifacts characteristic of a group. A shared idea that is part of the organizational culture can be the stated goal of $1 billion in sales for the next fiscal year or the sentiment on the poster in the stockroom that reads "The customer is always right." Examples of shared behaviors are the dress code that requires all employees to wear the company shirt, or the unwritten rule that employees are expected to arrive 30 minutes prior to the stated time of their floor shift. Shared material artifacts include, for example, stores or office buildings, and all the objects in them.

Frequently when I consider all the beliefs, behaviors, and artifacts in an organization, I find some contradictions that lead to employee confusion. In a company, examples of contradictory issues might be that company owners state that they put their employees first (a belief) but never meet the employees face to face (behavior) and provide no employee break room (material artifact). The employees experience a contradictory situation and are likely to suspect that the owners who never meet them and do not consider their needs for a break room do not really put employees first. In another example of a contradictory situation, the students at my university hear administrators say that students are their first priority but wonder, if that is the case, why student parking lots are the farthest from campus. One of the tasks of the anthropologist is to sort out all the conflicting cultural messages.

So, I see the organization *as* a culture and all the features of the organization—structure, reward system, rules of behavior, and goals—as components of the culture. However, no culture is a perfectly integrated, clearly bounded, and isolated entity. The company itself is a subculture within larger cultural units, the country in which its headquarters is located, for example. An organization is also a web of interacting cultures (see figure 2). Not only does the organization as a whole have a culture, but each department may have its own cultural components as well. Within the company, there are nested subcultures, such as educational software sales, which is nested inside software sales, which is nested inside general sales. Further, there are crosscutting cultural groupings, such as an administrative assistants' culture; these employees work in different departments (cultures) but their roles are similar, such that they form a cultural grouping that cuts across the organization. In addition, individuals are members of ethnic, regional, gender, and professional cultures outside of the organization, which contribute to the greater cultural picture.

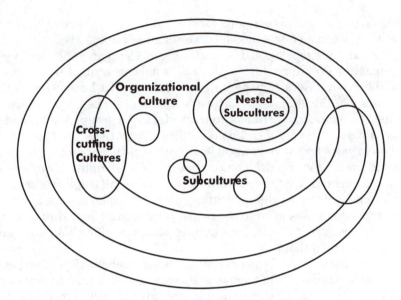

**Figure 2 Anthropological Perspective on Culture and
Organization**

The interrelated nature of the organization from my anthropological perspective is quite important in studying organizational culture. Anthropologically, it is important to study every group pattern. This can be demonstrated by comparing cultural universals with a list of important characteristics of an organization. A traditional view in anthropology is that every human culture includes a set of universal components: subsistence patterns, religion, an economic system, a political system, a language, social structure, and art. These universal components of culture are listed in the left-hand column of table 1. The right-hand column contains a list of important aspects of a business organization that parallel the universal components.

Anthropologically, each of these organizational topics is part of the cultural whole. Reward systems, for example, cannot be separated from organizational culture. They are in fact one set of ideas and behaviors that contribute to and are integrated with all other aspects of the culture. I study them as part of the culture's economic system. The organization chart, which essentially describes the structure of the organization, provides information about the political system. All these cultural universals represent components that interact. Much of this interaction is well documented in organization studies. For example, a political structure (organization structure) of hierarchical bureaucracy needs to fit the subsistence pattern (type of technology) of a slow-changing market. The strength of the anthropological concept of cul-

Table 1 Universal Components of Culture and Organizational Culture

Culture	Organizational Culture
Patterns of subsistence	Type of technology, division of labor
Religion and magic	Values, goals, ceremonies, myths
Economic system	Reward system
Political system	Organizational structure, leadership behavior, power and politics, conflict management
Language and communication	Communication
Social structure	Group formation other than formal organizational structure
Art	Organizational artifacts: dress, building type, logos

ture is that it views all these components as parts of the cultural whole, and therefore, they are potentially interrelated.

Most of the perceptions and behaviors typically associated with culture in the corporate-culture perspective that is found in the popular press equate to the universal component of magic and religion. That is, the component that includes values and goals and their accompanying ceremonies and myths.

INTERACTION OF DIVERSE CULTURES

An additional important insight that anthropology contributes to business is the understanding of how cultural groupings interface. One barrier to our ability as humans to understand the cultures of others is our tendency to mistake our own cultural behavior for natural, panhuman behavior. For example, feelings of affection are typical of all humans; they are panhuman. The manner in which affection is expressed, however, is cultural. The kiss is not universally accepted as a symbol of affection; some societies consider it suggestive of cannibalism. To give another example, for many people in the United States, eating three meals a day, one in the morning, at noon, and in the evening, is considered to be the correct schedule to give the body nourishment. However, few non-Western societies adhere to such an eating schedule. Many adhere to no schedules of any kind since clock time is cultural time and is not applicable in their cultures. The US eating schedule is a cultural definition of the appropriate time to eat in order to keep the body healthy, not a natural one.

Thus, each society views its own culturally sanctioned behaviors as *natural*. Pluralistic societies and multinational corporations afford workers many opportunities to view their own behavior as natural rather than cultural and to misunderstand other cultural groups in the workplace. Corporations with interests in multiple countries recognize the importance of understanding foreign cultures but frequently insist on doing things the way they are done at home even when on foreign soil. Thus, many organizational issues can be seen anthropologically as a problem in understanding diversity, where each cultural group views its own behavior as natural and therefore correct. One of the tasks of the anthropologist is to act as a culture broker and explain how each set of views is cultural, not natural.

Tomoko Hamada (1995) has studied the cultural misunderstandings involved in a sexual harassment charge brought by a female Euro-American worker against her Japanese manager in a Japanese-owned factory located in the United States. One of the acts of sexual harassment the female Euro-American worker cited was gift giving. Her manager had given her several gifts, such as bottles of liquor, which she interpreted as his expectation of sexual favors. The Japanese manager explained, however, that it is a Japanese custom to give gifts to good employees and that he gave gifts to several employees as recognition for their good work. Just as in the case of African American and Euro-American forms of address studied by Lee Baker, individuals in this case took a course of action based on certain cultural assumptions; different cultural assumptions stem from different cultural backgrounds. In the sexual harassment example, gift-giving actions were misinterpreted by the receiver because she did not share the same cultural assumption as the giver. The Japanese manager gave gifts (an action) with the Japanese cultural assumption that this action would be understood as a sign that he recognized good work. The Euro-American female worker was unaware of this Japanese cultural meaning and instead assumed a female Euro-American one, namely that the manager was interested in sexual favors. The anthropologist, again, can act as culture broker and sort out the misunderstandings that occur across cultural groupings.

Crucial to an anthropological understanding of cultural diversity is the process by which humans manipulate cultural symbols. Frequently, when the members of one culture borrow from the members of another, the borrowers recontextualize the borrowed feature to make it more useful in its new cultural surroundings. Products often take on new meaning. When Europeans first arrived on the North American continent, they were amazed and shocked by the ways of the aboriginal peoples. While most of what they witnessed was not understandable to them and of little use in their own lives, they did borrow some culture traits. Tobacco is a well-known example. For American Indians tobacco was sacred and was smoked during religious rituals. Sir Walter Raleigh recognized the usefulness of tobacco, transported it back to England, and the tobacco industry as we know it was born. While the Europeans borrowed the commodity, tobacco, from American Indians, they did not borrow the cultural context that surrounded the use of tobacco in the various tribes. Because the religious patterns did not fit into the European cultural patterns, none of them were borrowed.

In a study of consumer behavior, Jean-Marc Philibert and Christine Jourdan (1996) were able to identify the recontextualization of consumer goods among the people in the village of Erakor in the Republic of Vanuaru. Vanuaru, which gained its independence from Great Britain and France in 1980, is a string of islands in the South Pacific between the Solomon Islands and New Caledonia, with a population in 1995 of 150,000. The villagers of Erakor participated in long-held village patterns of subsistence based on horticulture and fishing. They sometimes worked as wage laborers in the nearby town of Vanuatu, where they also sold excess crops. In acquiring fishing rights, fields for crops, and land for houses, villagers exhibited a pattern of consumption in which commodities could not be bought and sold but were acquired through a pattern of mutual exchanges, gift-giving, or inheritance. By the 1970s, however, the villagers were participating in another pattern of consumption as well; they were buying services and manufactured goods for use in their home village. Such goods and services included refrigerators, cars, electricity, and concrete houses with single-purpose rooms, such as kitchens and bedrooms, and the appropriate furnishings for each room.

To an outsider from an industrial or postindustrial society, this might appear to be the addition of necessities to increase one's comfort. Philibert and Jourdan, however, noticed that many of these goods were not really needed, not well cared for, and were kept even after they broke. Working refrigerators were frequently only used to keep water cold and might not even be turned on unless a visitor was expected. (The villagers' traditional foods of tubers, green vegetables, rice, fruit, freshly baked bread, canned fish, freshly caught fish, and freshly purchased meat usually did not require refrigeration.) Sometimes even electric lights were not used at night as the household preferred the light of a hurricane lamp. Villagers also spent time sitting on mats in a traditional hut built in their yard rather than in their cement houses with living-room furniture. Why did the villagers go to all the work to earn enough wages to acquire these manufactured goods and services that they then did not use?

Philibert and Jourdan discovered that the reason was not the convenience or comfort these goods provided but their symbolic value in the system of social status. These goods linked the villagers with what they perceived to be the outside world and proved their social equality with Europeans as well as their social superiority over villages on other islands with less access to wage labor and manufactured goods. Philibert and Jourdan point out that the villagers exhibited agency in that they, not outsiders, determined the value of these goods in their lives. This pattern cannot be understood as one forced on them by the outside world but instead as one they created themselves. To understand this system, Philibert and Jourdan had to come to understand the recontextualization of borrowed cultural artifacts and behaviors among the villagers of Erakor (Philibert and Jourdan 1996:55–76).

The Japanese creators of the Walkman originally designed it to have two sets of headphones because from a Japanese cultural perspective it was rude to "tune out" and listen to music by oneself. The reason the Walkman was eventually sold in the West with one set of headphones was because its Japanese manufacturers understood individualism in the West where listeners were less interested in sharing and more interested in personal satisfaction (Classen and Howes 1996:185).

Savvy product development specialists like the Turkish migrants to Germany and the Japanese manufacturers of the Walkman pay close attention to culture in markets they wish to penetrate. In marketing and product design, understanding the value of culture borrowing is crucial.

In organizations, culture borrowing—such as when technology that is developed and used in one country is transferred to a plant in another country—is important as well. Implementing the technology, created according to standards common in one culture, often can be problematic in the new environment. Tomoko Hamada found this in her study of the transfer to Japan of a North American process for producing plastic wrap.

Through a joint venture arrangement, a factory was built in Japan based on the technology used in the United States. While the Japanese and North Americans both put much effort into transferring this technology, there were several glitches. For example, the Japanese redesigned the arrangement of the machines on the factory floor because their factory floor space was smaller than the North American factory floor space. Space is at a premium in Japan. The Americans had not thought to explain the reason for the wide spacing of the machines.

It never occurred to them that the Japanese would not follow their floor plan exactly. Because of the tighter spacing in the Japanese factory and the fact that the building was not well sealed against dust, the machines got dirty faster. The Japanese were not aware that they had to clean the machines frequently, and the plastic wrap the factory produced had an unacceptable number of blemishes caused by dirt. While the problems were eventually worked out, a lack of communication about the importance of space between machines and their need for cleaning initially caused the technology to produce an imperfect product (Hamada 1991).

CONCLUSION

In this chapter, we looked at the construct of *culture* to understand how anthropologists use it in business. One of the ways it is used is in looking at cultural groupings. The firefighters and the not-for-profit managers discussed in this chapter are examples of professional cultural groupings. The terms of address common for African Americans and Euro-Americans and the housing styles popular with Italian Canadians are characteristics of ethnic cultural groupings. The sexual harassment case involving a male Japanese manager and an American female worker, where regional groupings and gender groupings got tangled, is an example of the cultural complexity that is typical of modern organizational life. In each case, the anthropologist is looking for behavior, beliefs, and products that are characteristic of a group and learned over time. By looking for these patterns, researchers see the groupings in a way that allows them to apply anthropological theory.

We also looked at how the construct of culture is used in marketing, consumer behavior, and product design. We discussed what Howes terms the "creolization" of the world, where commodities flow around the world and are adopted in new areas in proportion to their cultural usefulness, even though the new uses might be ones the original producers never imagined. Recognizing patterned behavior is valuable in product design as well. The Walkman was designed to fit Western behavior patterns.

The comments of John Bennett are appropriate for the way in which anthropologists study culture when applied to business. As an anthropologist, one is "an expert on the patterned aspects of group behavior" (Bennett 1954:171). One is doing what James Clifford suggests that "fieldworkers have always done, building up social wholes ('culture' in the American tradition) through a concentration on significant elements" (Clifford 1989:63).

Endnote

[1] To further understand the variety of definitions of culture and critiques of them, see Kroeber and Kluckhohn 1952, Gamst and Norbeck 1976, and Marcus and Fischer 1986. Anthropologists approach their research from a variety of theoretical and conceptual positions. Consequently, not all anthropologists will agree with this presentation of the anthropological perspective. The perspective used here is one the author has found useful in understanding behavior in complex organizations but should not be considered descriptive of the entire field of anthropology. For a more thorough discussion of the variety in and historical development of theory and method in anthropology, see Harris 1968; Borofsky 1993; Salzman 2001; and Garbarino 1977/1983.

Chapter Five

Ethical Concerns

The importance of being professional . . .

In the 1980s the anthropology community was deeply involved in a debate over ethics (discussed in chapter 2). At the crux of the argument was the question of whether being paid by an employer for the information in studies conducted by professional anthropologists was ethical. Many anthropologists feel there is a dangerous possibility that the rights of the individuals who are the subjects of the studies are in jeopardy when anthropologists are hired by clients, be they government agencies or corporations, to use their expertise to find out information for these clients.

Suppose corporate executives hire an anthropologist to find out why their employees are not performing their jobs according to the expectations of the corporate executives, and they want the anthropologist to explain how to get the employees to do what the executives want. Could the information gleaned from this research be damaging to the employees being studied? Or, suppose corporate executives hire an anthropologist to devise a marketing plan for a new product. Will this research assist the corporation in convincing people to buy a product that they don't need and is harmful, thereby increasing corporate profit at the expense of the consumer? Is it ethical for the anthropologist to do this? What if this research is to be kept secret (a common requirement when one is hired to do research by a corporation)? Is it ethical for the anthropologist to engage in secret research?

As professionals, anthropologists must consider the important ethical implications of these questions. The issue of the appropriateness of secret research is rooted in the ethical issues anthropologists faced in the 1960s and 1970s, described in chapter 2. The American

Anthropological Association (AAA) wanted to make clear that spying was unethical activity for professional anthropologists. Related to that issue was a second one concerning the rights of research subjects. During most of its history, the anthropological community has strongly defended the rights of research subjects and the responsibility of the researcher to prevent her subjects from being harmed by the research. The clandestine research episodes in the 1960s and 1970s were heinous because they violated these basic principles. Moreover, these episodes left anthropologists with a distaste for work in which the researcher is paid by an organization for gathering data that will not be made public. As discussed in chapter 2, by the 1980s many anthropologists were working for hire. Because the AAA determined that this new work for hire was not harmful, it revised its code of ethics to allow professional anthropologists to conduct proprietary research.

In 2007 another ethical controversy shook the profession. The US military had initiated a new program called the Human Terrain System (HTS) in the fall of 2006. In this program, five-person teams of social scientists and intelligence specialists were deployed with combat brigades in Iraq and Afghanistan. The social scientists served as cultural advisors and reported to the brigade commander and his senior staff. Their espoused goal was to provide cultural information about Afghan and Iraqi civilians that could save lives by educating the troops about cultural misunderstandings and cultural norms of behavior. The military understood the value of anthropological training and was recruiting anthropologists for these teams. Several anthropologists served in this capacity.

In 2007, there was an uproar at the AAA annual meeting about the ethics of this kind of work. Concerns were multiple. It was questionable whether voluntary informed consent, an ethical requirement for anthropological study, could be obtained in the fog of war and in the power imbalance present when the researcher is embedded with occupying forces. There was further concern that the fieldwork might be used to harm individuals the anthropologists studied; for example, the data could be used as part of military intelligence to target people the military deemed were enemies rather than innocent civilians. This would violate the AAA ethical principle to do no harm to those one studies.

In fact, the database developed through this project would be available to numerous audiences beyond the brigade commander, which could include the US Central Intelligence Agency and the governments of both Iraq and Afghanistan (Beyerstein 2007). The anthropologists would have no control over these uses of their data. A committee charged by the AAA Executive Board with reviewing the ethical concerns about this work determined in its 2008 report that working with the HTS program "can no longer be considered a legitimate professional exercise of anthropology" (American Anthropological Association CEAUSSIC).

At this writing, the AAA is considering a revision of its current ethics code, which has been in effect since 1998. The proposed new code renews the anthropological emphasis on doing no harm and stresses that this must include thinking through the "unintended consequences and long-term impacts" of one's work. It also stresses that researchers must avoid research in which "consent may not be truly voluntary or informed." The current Code of Ethics clearly states that research that fulfills the code's "expectations is ethical, regardless of the source of funding (public or private) or purpose (i.e., 'applied,' 'basic,' 'pure,' or 'proprietary')" (American Anthropological Association 1998). While not banning proprietary research, it states anthropologists should not normally withhold research results from research participants when those results are shared with others and that such research raises "complex ethical questions" that should be carefully considered (American Anthropological Association Draft).

Today professional anthropologists operate under several codes of ethics. Those most important in North America are the codes of the AAA (http://www.aaanet.org/committees/ethics/ethcode/htm), the Society for Applied Anthropology (SfAA) (http://www.sfaa.net/sfaaethic.html), and the National Association for the Practice of Anthropology (NAPA) (http://www.aaanet.org/napa/code.htm). Taken together, these codes establish a valuable set of criteria for the consultant to follow. They cannot possibly, however, address all potential ethical conflicts an anthropologist may experience.

THINKING THROUGH THE ETHICAL CONSEQUENCES OF A PROJECT

For the business anthropologist, the first task is to think through the proposed project and determine if it is harmful to the individuals who are the subjects of the study. In marketing, consumer behavior, and product design, for example, an overriding concern is the potential harm of the product for which one is being asked to develop a design or a marketing strategy. If the individual anthropologist judges that this product is harmful to those who will consume it, then the anthropologist is bound by our ethical codes to reject the project. This is because those who will consume it are research subjects, and an anthropologist must not cause harm to research subjects.

In some cases consumer research seems clearly ethical. If an anthropologist is asked to provide design guidance for a new software package intended for a particular market niche, chemists, for example, and having such a package makes the chemists' job easier, then studying chemists' research behavior in order to design the package effectively seems harmless. In other cases, the harmless factor is less clear. Improving marketing strategies for a product people do not really need may seem less desirable. Are the purchasers who are the subjects of the study harmed if they are convinced to buy a product when they never knew they needed it before? This simply increases corporate profit at the expense of the little guy, does it not? Are consumers all that easily brainwashed into buying things they do not need, and if so, is it the anthropologist's responsibility to protect consumers from themselves? Is it patronizing of the anthropologist to decide for others what they do and do not need? These are all questions each anthropologist must answer on a case-by-case basis. The primary responsibility is clear enough: anthropologists should not cause harm to those who are the subjects of their studies. In real life, however, applying this ethical rule is difficult. Each anthropologist must think through the issues in each case and reject those projects she feels are harmful.

In the case of business consulting, some researchers fear that providing managers with ethnographic data on their employees assists the managers in manipulating employees. In my work in organizational culture, for example, I have had managers ask me, "How can I use culture as a lever to change behavior?" When managers use such language, I suspect that they are interested in the possibility of manipulating culture. I believe, however, that the danger of effecting this kind of manipulation is minimal because culture is not a set of behavior patterns that a manager can decree; it is something that all employees create and transmit; it is a complicated process that is difficult to direct. The long history of applied work in anthropology attests to the difficulty of trying to force people to change. Thus, while we must be ever-aware of protecting the rights of all subjects, we most likely do not have to be on guard against culture manipulation.

Instead, anthropologists in their role as broker between organizational units can provide employees and executives with a mutual understanding by listening to and talking with individuals employed at all levels in the organization. More than other types of business consultants, anthropologists understand that all members of the organization, including those at lower levels, must be heard for the organization to be understood, thereby legitimating and valuing the views of these employees. Often these voices are brought into the discussion for the first time.

The business anthropologist has the opportunity to negotiate the terms of the research agreement in advance of the work. Thus, ethical concerns can be identified and included in the research design, and potential problems or misunderstandings can be eliminated. If expectations are clarified at the outset, feelings of frustration and animosity can be avoided. Consider the following case: Kanu Kogod (1994) faced difficulties in a project for Green & Black, Inc., a small company that had recently grown to just over 100 employees. With that growth came diversity; although white males owned the company, approximately 25 percent of the workforce consisted of African Americans, Filipino Americans, and other Asian Americans, and about 50 percent the workforce were women, with three serving on the 12-member board. All of this diversity engendered allegations of discrimination and reverse discrimination.

Kogod and her colleagues were hired to help the company become more diversity friendly. As the work progressed, Kogod found herself having difficulty defining her "client." She had multiple potential clients: the managing partner (Tom), the owners, the executive committee, the organization as a whole, and the "powerless." This last group represented the workers whose voice was not heard. As an anthropologist, she felt particularly compelled to champion this group. This was not the group that hired her, however, and the issue of client identity was so compelling it almost stopped the project after several rounds of butting heads with Tom over the project's scope. She wanted to help the powerless, but providing this type of guidance was not part of the original project, although it would be useful in addressing the organizational problems uncovered by her study.

Tom wanted her to stick with the original scope of the project. Whether she did so or not depended on who her client was. If it were Tom, then she must adhere to his preferences. If not Tom, then who was it and who would decide the scope? Finally, she wrote a 12-page memo to the two owners stating all the issues she had uncovered. The outcome? It became clear that Tom was the client and he had the power to determine the scope of the project. However, the memo was so insightful that it helped Tom to see ways in which Kogod's suggestions for expanding the project were appropriate. In addition, Kogod came to understand better the workings of power in this organization. The work on her project went more smoothly from that point on. This case emphasizes the need to be clear about expectations. The best time to do so is in the beginning, when constructing the contract, but sometimes issues arise during the work that require the anthropologist to ask for a reassessment of the conditions of the work (Kogod 1995).

ANONYMITY ISSUES

The question of maintaining subjects' anonymity is important when conducting research in all areas of business. In marketing, consumer behavior, and product design anthropologists typically provide their clients with a report not only rich in descriptive text but also one that contains photographs or video clips of subjects whose stories are shared in the report. While the purpose of such stories and the accompanying photos is to underscore the findings of the report, design anthropologists have found that pictures of subjects can take on a life of their own. While the anthropologist gets consent from the informant to use his story and picture in presentations and reports, neither the anthropologist nor the informant expects the company to use the photo for other purposes. However, in the fast-paced marketing world, someone can remember an image from a presentation and throw that image into an ad campaign. Suddenly, the informant's face appears on a poster or on billboards all over town, something for which he never gave consent. This is an important and dangerous ethical problem for the anthropologist who originally supplied the picture. This problem must be addressed specifically in the contractual arrangements with clients.

When it is desired by the subjects, anonymity must be protected at both the organizational level and the individual level. Corporate executives often insist on anonymity for the organization in any work the anthropologist may publish. This is frequently the only way they will allow the anthropologist to publish the results of work done in their corporation because they may fear that some aspects of that work may place the organization in an unfavorable light. If they desire anonymity and have negotiated it, then the anthropologist must honor the commitment he has made.

Since the corporation is a study subject requiring protection just as individuals in the corporation are, this has caused problems for me as a consultant and an academic researcher. In one study I negotiated up front an agreement that I would be able to publish any of the research I conducted in the organization without censure of my findings as long as I did not identify the company. Not identifying the company included not providing details in my descriptions that would allow readers to guess the company's identity. The challenge here was that anthropological work is replete with rich description, but that same rich description could give away the company's identity. Company executives reviewed my writings for identity issues. Eventually we came to an agreement on the amount of detail I was allowed to publish. It made my published work less rich in description than I would have liked, but it did not alter the detailed explanation of my findings.

Protecting anonymity of individual informants in the organization can be difficult. Even when one has insured their anonymity contractually at the beginning of the project, problems often arise. If one quotes employees, albeit anonymously, in written reports, it is sometimes possible for others to guess who the authors of the quotes are. The outside researcher, who does not know these individuals personally, may innocently quote statements containing phraseology that only one individual in the corporation is known to use and thus unwittingly identify that individual. For example, I was interviewing in a corporation in which executives assured me that anonymity was of the utmost

importance. No one would talk to me otherwise. On more than one occasion, an informant told me not to quote a particular part of the conversation in my report. One individual said, "They are trinket junkies,
that is the best way to describe them, but don't use the term 'trinket
junkies' in your report. They will know it came from me."

Another danger occurs when describing real situations in the
workplace. The anthropologist may describe work procedures that are
in violation of company policy and cause the company to take actions
against a group of workers, even though individual anonymity is maintained. William Graves and Mark Shields describe just such an incident. An ethnographic study of work patterns and use of information
resources among staff in a university-support organization revealed
work processes in violation of standard procedure (Graves and Shields
1991). One administrator who received the report challenged the
researcher and insisted he reveal his sources with regard to this violation. When he would not, the administrator went down on the shop floor
and demanded to know the identity of relevant staff. In this case, while
identities were never revealed as far as the researcher is aware, the
interviewees were not as fully protected from harm as the researcher
had intended. How does the consultant know whether revealing such
violations of standards will result in (1) the implementation of improved
standards or (2) punitive action toward the violators? Anthropologists
must constantly be alert to the problems of protecting subjects.

COLLEAGUES AS INFORMANTS

Other issues arise in upholding the anthropological ethic of not
harming informants. Some anthropologists work at the organization
they are studying. Diana Forsythe worked for ten years in labs involved
in software production, and part of her responsibility was to study her
own workplace. She describes a thorny ethical issue:

> One of the main goals of scientists and graduate students in labo-
> ratory settings is access to limited resources; these include money,
> promotion, space, and the attention of people senior to oneself. As a
> fieldworker, I would wish to help my informants to achieve such
> goals, or at least not to impede them. But as a fellow lab member, I
> sometimes found myself in direct competition with them. Students
> and researchers assigned to carrels in loud, busy rooms wanted
> their own offices; I wanted an office, too. Lab members wanted the
> lab head to read and comment upon their papers; I wanted his at-
> tention, too, for my own proposals and papers. And when I discov-
> ered that I was being paid two-thirds of what a male scientist ten
> years my junior was making, I wanted a raise. (Forsythe 1999:9)

Forsythe goes on to describe a particularly sticky situation in which a senior researcher, one of the subjects of her study, verbally attacked her in lab meetings. Should her ethical code not to harm subjects prevent her from fighting back? If she fought back, could she use information she gained through her study and would not have known otherwise? In a different situation, she applied for a job at another institution, and several of her colleagues at her current job, who were subjects in her study, wrote letters of recommendation for her. In traditional fieldwork, it is unusual to need one's research subjects to write letters of recommendation (Forsythe 1999:9–10).

Forsythe is describing the blurring of boundaries caused when one works for the people one studies. While this situation does create some sticky issues, I expect to see it occur more frequently. All anthropologists are struggling with the issues of the boundaries between researcher and subject and discovering that the boundaries are less clear than we previously thought. Working for or with the informant is just one more example of this muddy boundary issue and of the complexity and tension that have always been present in the researcher–subject interaction.

Jennifer Croissant describes a related thorny problem. She worked in a research institution studying researchers and teachers of neurophysiology, motor control, biomechanics, and rehabilitation engineering and the design methodologies and assumptions they employed. She posed the question: "Is it ever legitimate to criticize those whom one studies?" If not, then how can she provide a constructive critique? Under what conditions is such criticism acceptable? Croissant cites the following example: One of her students mentioned another class at the institution in which engineering students were given the task of redesigning night vision goggles for the US Border Patrol. At no time in that class were the ethical issues of designing such goggles discussed, and students were given no choice but to participate. Croissant felt the instructor should have held a discussion about ethics.

Croissant saw at least four possible positions regarding the ethical nature of this project: (1) the border needs protection, (2) border agents might find people more quickly and save lives, (3) those who escort people across the border might successfully use these to avoid border agents, and (4) the students/engineers should just do their job and stay out of ethical issues about products they develop. None of these positions were discussed in the class in which the assignment was given. In her constructive critique of the practices at this institution, should Croissant criticize the instructor, who was both her subject and her colleague, for not discussing ethics? Croissant came to the conclusion as a result of this and other instances: "It is not clear to me that we should never impede our informant's goals" (Croissant 1999:25). This is a conclusion others working in organizations might reach as well.

ALL ANTHROPOLOGISTS
FACE ETHICAL PROBLEMS

Many of the stickier ethical questions in consulting for business are shared with other areas of applied anthropology. For example, if an anthropologist helps change a job requirement, has he harmed an employee who cannot adjust to the change? That dilemma is similar to the one faced by an anthropologist who helps change production techniques in rural Guatemala. Has she harmed an individual who cannot adjust? If the anthropologist helps raise productivity in the workplace (whether that workplace be in an American corporation or an African village), workers may be displaced. Has the anthropologist behaved ethically?

The presence of these ethical issues does not require us to ban applied work no matter whether the setting is a consumer's living room, a large corporation, or a small South American village. It does require us to move into the work with awareness and caution and keep the ethical questions always in our minds. These are issues with which all anthropologists must wrestle, no matter what form their research takes. The old notion that anthropologists should stay out of their informants' lives to avoid ethical entanglements is not an ethically neutral stance. Today, indigenous populations are increasingly viewing this stance as ethically questionable, for in their eyes it reflects an unwillingness to help the population from which the anthropologist gained so much experience and information. For example, how can an anthropologist work with American Indians today and not be an advocate for the changes they desire?

Additionally, there are few nonliterate populations left who are uninterested in the manner in which their comments are included in published work (Fluehr-Lobban 1991). Debates on intellectual property are bringing to the fore the question of ownership of knowledge. Even in traditional areas of anthropological inquiry, the research subjects are raising questions about the ethical nature of the anthropologists' practice of protecting their subjects' identities while making careers of publishing their worldviews. The view of research subjects as passive and powerless and in need of our protection has given way to one of subjects who are active participants in an interactive research process in which they are involved in the design and outcome of the work. Researchers can no longer hide their work from the subjects, nor can they dismiss the subjects' criticisms as a simple reflection of the insider's difficulty in seeing his own culture clearly. The subjects, whether they are corporate employees or indigenous communities, are holding the researcher accountable for the contents of her reports.

CONCLUSION

In this new age for anthropology, all research is interactive. Like all anthropologists, those working in business are required to consider the ethical implications of all their work, consult the professional codes of ethics, and decline work that would be unethical according to those codes. As John Sherry states regarding his consumer research work at Intel:

> While I cannot claim ten million potential [Intel] customers as "my tribe," I would still hope to be an advocate for the interests of real people, the potential technology consumers, and to be honest about the potential effects, both positive and negative, that new technologies may bring (while understanding that such forecasting is a notoriously risky undertaking). (Sherry 1999:20)

Chapter Six

Marketing and
Consumer Behavior

Big hair and Barbie dolls . . .

Why has one London-based firm been successful at cornering the market on supplying salted peanuts to consumers in Trinidad? Daniel Miller (1997) learned the answer. Trinidadians prefer shiny peanuts. The London supplier discovered that Chinese peanuts are shiny and, therefore, imported peanuts to Trinidad primarily from China, rather than from other countries. In Japan, canned baby food is typically not a hot-selling item because the Japanese prefer fresh food and because Japanese mothers are expected to prepare fresh meals for their children. How did Gerber manage to make a place for itself selling its baby food in Japan? As Millie Creighton learned, Gerber's baby foods were introduced in Japan by a Japanese company, Meijiya, and were marketed not as a time-saving device but as a valuable education tool. In Japan, education is highly valued, and mothers are responsible for seeing that their young children receive all the right stimulation for learning. Gerber's baby foods were packaged and marketed as education lessons for infants, and each container had an education lesson for the child printed on the label. For example, lesson 4 for infants age six to seven months "involved achieving the state at which taste preferences in food begin to develop" (Creighton 1994:36).

Will people use hand lotion and tissues at the office as well as at home? Sue Squires (2002) conducted research for a manufacturer of personal care products. The client wanted to know if people would use its personal care products at the office as well as in the home, which is the traditional setting for such use. Through observation and interviews, she and her colleagues learned that people did not want to use these products at the office in front of other people, even though they wanted to use them during the workday. Some personal-use products had made the transition to the public area of the office, however. These included hand lotion and tissues, which were displayed in designer containers, making them more appropriate in appearance for the office. The containers no longer represented the home and the bathroom. Squires's recommendation was not to develop new products but to repackage the existing ones in office friendly ways.

John F. Sherry explains that, from an anthropological perspective, *consumer behavior* can be viewed as an adaptive strategy shaping an individual's quality of life. So all of us as consumers use our consumption as a way to adapt. In addition, *marketing* from an anthropological perspective, is a directed intervention strategy of planned change (Sherry 1995). The marketer's goal is to increase sales of a product. To do so requires more purchases of the product. The marketer is attempting to change cultural norms so that more people buy the product. If this happens, the cultural norms have been successfully changed. Thus, from an anthropological perspective, the marketer's strategy is to implement planned change successfully.

For the anthropologist, marketing and consumption are important forces in human behavior worldwide, and understanding these forces is essential to understanding political economy and world systems. Anthropologists view consumer behavior in a cultural, historical, and global context. As Rita Denny (2002:148) of Practica Group explains, "My work is in decoding the meaning of brands, bringing the consumers of products and services to life as cultural beings, understanding the role of products, brands or services in the context of everyday life, where meaning is produced and consumed. It is at heart a cultural analysis."

Advertisers and marketing managers can use anthropological methods to get closer to the consumer and to gain greater understanding of consumer needs and product uses. Denny explains that advertising agencies have to determine the best way to market products that have changed as the world has changed. The rapid change in technology, which is so much a part of our lives today, means that consumers need to think about old products in new contexts. For example, a telephone is not just for talking anymore. The use of a telephone 20 years ago is quite different from the use of a "telephone" today when families are likely to have multiple phones and when a phone can also be a computer, a game console, an Internet conduit, or a camera. Furthermore, a phone is no longer tied to hardwired connections and can go wherever its user goes. In addition to keeping up with rapid changes in technology, as new markets emerge around the world, increasing sales of a product frequently means taking the product to those new markets.

Advertisers and marketers must understand the needs and worldview of the consumers in each of these markets; the product must be marketed differently in each.

Many products face competition from similar products, and a product must somehow distinguish itself from all the others that perform the same function. For example, when purchasing a cell phone, which one do you buy? Brand names have become even more important as a means of distinguishing among similar products. Making sure that consumers constantly and consistently recognize the product's name is an ongoing task of the marketer. All of these marketing issues and more now face the product marketer (Denny 2002). Anthropological methods provide new tools for attacking these issues.

ANTHROPOLOGICAL THEORY AND PRACTICE IN MARKETING AND CONSUMER BEHAVIOR

Anthropologists have rediscovered the importance of material culture in understanding human behavior. Material culture is the physical objects (called artifacts) that a cultural group produces and utilizes, and includes everything from houses and tools to clothing and medicine. Arjun Appadurai's (1986) call for a renewed focus on the circulation of commodities in social life has been heeded by anthropologists working in business. While the traditional focus in anthropology has been on the *type* of exchange, Appadurai suggests that focusing on the *object* of the exchange allows for a new understanding of human behavior. For example, in the Trobriand Islands in a ritual known in anthropology as the Kula ring, men traditionally practiced an exchange of religiously significant objects. Men moved from island to island exchanging shell necklaces and armbands with specific trading partners. When anthropologists focus on the details of how the exchange is carried out, they focus on the type of exchange. When they focus on the necklaces and armbands and the creation, movements, and uses of a specific necklace, they focus on the object of exchange.

As Grant McCracken (1988) suggests, consumption, from the viewpoint of an anthropologist, is the processes at work when consumer goods are created, bought, and used, and understanding consumption is important to understanding culture. Daniel Miller (1998) suggests that in our theoretical understanding of the processes at work in society, anthropologists have been slow to recognize the key role of consumption. Therefore, anthropologists working in the field of consumer behavior not only provide insights that are useful to their clients but also make a substantial contribution to anthropological theory.

The study of material culture plays a new role in the work of anthropologists as we recognize how humans use material goods to construct their own identities and the identities of others. McCracken (1995) is interested in how people use consumer goods to construct their concepts of self and the world. For example, he explains the importance of consumer goods by analyzing hairstyles that hair products allow us to create.

To gain his knowledge, he spent hours observing in beauty salons and taking notes on what he saw and heard. He listened in on conversations between hairstylists and their customers about what color of hair dye and which haircut would create the client's desired impression. He also conducted interviews with both hairdressers and their clients and analyzed advertising and popular culture publications. His research took 18 months to complete and involved working in Atlanta, Chicago, Dallas, Los Angeles, New York, San Francisco, Seattle, and Toronto. The hairdressers he interviewed were both male and female. Interviewees talked about big hair, for instance, which is that cap of teased and sprayed hair that stands out from the head, which we have all seen on personalities like Dolly Parton. It "speaks" to create an identity as a person who is forthright, gregarious, and full of gumption.

McCracken (1996:113) used archives of popular magazine and newspaper articles and advertisements to trace the advertising history of hairstyles and colors. For example, articles depict how dyeing one's hair in the 1950s could get a woman derogatorily labeled a "bottle blonde." Lawrence Gelb, president of Clairol, began advertising his product as a "tint," not a "dye," in order to make coloring one's hair seem less scandalous. Through magazine articles, McCracken traces the change in attitude toward dyed hair that occurred in the 1960s. One interesting aspect of McCracken's study is that the subject matter is women's hair only because he found that men would not talk about their hair.

McCracken learned how women use hair color and style to create the image of self that they wish to project to the world. The "dress for success" look for women, which began in the late 1970s, is an example of how consumer goods can be used to create an image of self. Women entering the world of business professionals were a marginalized group in the 1970s. Thus, in their dress they appropriated some of the characteristics of the "power" group of business professionals—males. Women dressed in suits with jackets cut like those of men's jackets and frequently wore bows, scarves, or actual ties at the neck to approximate a man's tie. Women were using consumer goods to create and transform their image of self (McCracken 1988, 1995:126–127).

McCracken also explains how people "displace" ideals that are important to them (such as a harmonious family life) and use consumer goods as a way to both protect and reach those ideals. The success of advertising campaigns that tie consumer products to small-town, early twentieth-century living are marketing examples that make use of our tendency to "displace." Bread that is advertised as being just like your grandmother used to bake and the real estate developer's advertisement of his suburban housing development as a rural community are examples of the use of displacement in ads. McCracken also describes how we collect consumer goods into a grouping that represents a particular idea. What are the assorted goods that identify a "yuppie," for example? McCracken's point is that consumer goods, then, have symbolic properties. We use consumption to create and re-create our identities. Consumer processes are important processes at work in contemporary society.

Patricia Sunderland and Rita Denny explain the importance of metaphor as a "key analytic and strategic tool" (2007:93). In a study of the meaning of drugs for US tweens (young people aged 10–13), they found the tweens talked about marijuana in terms of plants and about other drugs in terms of chemicals. It was the latter they considered the most harmful and did not consider the plant, marijuana, as harmful unless laced with other (chemical) drugs. In addition, they considered cigarettes and alcohol to be drugs but worried not about their harmfulness but about their damage to the body; for example, cigarettes caused yellow teeth and bad breath. Thus Sunderland and Denny recommended advertizing campaigns that focused on the metaphors of damage and chemicals to fight drug use among tweens. They further pointed out the difficulty in combating marijuana use in that it was identified with the metaphor of plants, considered wholesome, organic, and natural. An anthropological understanding of symbols and metaphors is valuable in consumer research.

Negotiated Identity

How loaded with meaning is a Barbie doll? Very loaded, according to Elizabeth Chin, who studied toy use by poor and working-class, African American, ten-year-olds in New Haven, Connecticut. Chin observed children's behavior, taped her conversations with them, and photographed them with their toys. She enriched her understanding of the social significance of toys by studying other published work on toys, one of which is Erica Rand's *Barbie's Queer Accessories* (1995). She considered relevant advertisements, such as the stories on the packaging of many products sold by Olmec toys, started in the mid-1980s by Yla Eason because she couldn't find a black superhero for her son. While Olmec is no longer manufacturing toys, Eason's stories informed Chin of the experiences that caused Eason to become a minority toy maker.

When Mattel first started making the Barbie doll (1959), she was white. In 1967 Mattel made the first African American Barbie, but she lacked African American features other than dark skin., Black Barbie was launched in 1980, but she still had white features. The reason behind the production of ethnically correct fashion dolls was to raise young girls' self-esteem by providing them with dolls that look like they do. Chin found, however, that the ten-year-olds in her study were more likely to possess a white Barbie, suggesting that Mattel's efforts were ineffectual in some neighborhoods because dark-skinned dolls were not available in stores that were accessible to the consumers for whom they were created. So the children renegotiated their Barbie's identity by styling her hair in African American styles using beads, braids, and foil. The consumers, the girls themselves, were resourceful in using hairstyles to create a product that was unavailable to them.

In their cross-cultural study of beauty pageants, Colleen Cohen, Richard Wilk, and Beverly Stoeltje (1996:231–232) suggest that there is a world industry devoted to creating culture. In beauty pageants worldwide, certain characteristics, such as being tall and thin, have been identified and foregrounded as important distinctions to recognize. These characteristics are essentialized, while others are ignored or backgrounded. In this kind of a situation, beauty has become a commodity and those defining it on the world stage are culture producers of the global commodity, beauty, while the rest of us become the consumers of the commodified culture they have created. The industry has defined what beauty is and what differences will be recognized, and the consumer is free to express his opinion only within the confines of the categories of difference set up by the industry. In Belize, for example, the local standard of beauty is a woman who is short with large hips and thighs. While an individual like that might win Miss Belize, she would not win Miss World.

Resistance through Consumption

As consumers, do we determine what we will consume? How easily are we influenced by "Madison Avenue" and those fancy ad campaigns? Do we really make our own decisions? The beauty study just described suggests that we do not make our own decisions. Anthropologists working on issues surrounding consumer behavior, however, find that we both direct and are directed by others. Daniel Miller (1998) points out that consumer response to the introduction of New Coke is a prime example of successful consumer resistance to the dictates of a powerful multinational corporation. Although Coca-Cola test-marketed the changed formula of its flagship drink, and found that "people chose the new formula 55 percent of the time, and the original one 45 percent of the time," when New Coke replaced traditional Coke on store shelves, consumers resisted buying it. Apparently they did not like the taste of New Coke and also had an emotional connection to the original product (Food Inc. 2009). The corporation quickly got the message as sales figures dropped, and it reinstituted the traditional formula adding the word "Classic" in 1985 to the Coca-Cola label. Consumers responded with their wallets, and the company experienced a significant gain in sales. In 2009, Coke removed "Classic" from its logo because, according to *Beverage Digest* Editor John Sicher, "classic doesn't sound youthful and contemporary" (quoted in Food Inc. 2009).

Steven Kates and Russell Belk found that a more complex situation can exist when consumers show their resistance by consuming. Through observation of Lesbian and Gay Pride Day celebrations in Toronto over a four-year period and through interviews with gay men who participated in the festivals, Kates and Belk found that Pride Day celebrants used consumption to voice their resistance to political and social forces opposed to the homosexual lifestyle. The parade and accompanying week of activities drew some 700,000 people in 1996.

Marketers had targeted gay and lesbian shoppers with products that express resistance, but the parade participants complained that the festival had become too commercialized by vendors of food, clothing, jewelry, and other goods and services and by travel agents who marketed trips to Pride Day celebrations in cities across North America. Despite their complaints, attendees bought many commercial items during the celebration. Celebrants ate and drank in nearby restaurants and attended dances the night before the parade. On parade day, they ate and drank at the open-air beer gardens and roadside food stands and bought merchandise from the street vendors selling cards, books, T-shirts, jewelry, and sexual accoutrements. Purchases included T-shirts with slogans like "Nobody knows that my boyfriend is gay" and "Shh! I'm gay, but don't tell anyone," as well as leatherman gingerbread cookies and rainbow-colored flags. Gays and lesbians were using their consumption to express resistance, by choosing gay shops and vendors rather than mainstream shops and vendors (Kates and Belk 2001).

Experiential Consumption

> "As soon as you push off that beach, at the put-in where you start your river trip, it's magical. It really is. That's where the river magic comes in. It's like you go through this door, and you close it when it goes behind ya."

> "I totally agree with the spiritual thing. . . . I love it. I love it in the wilderness anywhere, but for some reason on the river. . . . I mean, humans are drawn to the water." (Quotes from river guides in Arnould, Price, and Otnes 1999:43, 50)

It is not just products that we buy; there is a growing consumer market for "experience," and anthropologists have documented the ways in which this market works. Eric Arnould and Linda Price studied the consumption of "extraordinary experience" in their research on white-water river rafting. For example, in 1995 they conducted research on the Yampa and Green Rivers in Utah and Colorado, focusing on both the rafting companies and the consumers. They conducted in-depth interviews with 15 river guides, conducted a post-trip survey with over 50 customers of five-day rafting trips, and did 10 days of participant observation of white-water river rafting.

They suggest that what the rafting companies are selling is an experience, enhanced by the rhetoric of the river guides (which evokes images and feelings that assist in creating the experience), as the quotes above suggest. In a five-day rafting trip, guides introduce the participants to magic. They speak of the river in a reverential manner, emphasizing the need to respect it and the importance of cooperation among the group. They compare the experience of being on the river, which transcends the forces of man-made time, with the participants' regular, everyday world. The potential of danger involved in white-water rafting and the accompanying fear, along with the natural setting so far from the participants' regular world, all combine to provide a near religious or magical experience for the participants. The consumers purchase an experience.

Millie Creighton provides examples of consuming experiences in Japan. In a country that is highly urbanized and industrialized, there is a yearning for the small, rural village of one's ancestors. The tourism industry sells consumers this form of nostalgia, the experience of returning home to rural villages. In many cases, the return is not to one's actual village but to other villages in remote areas that suggest the idyllic life of an earlier time. In addition, *furusato* (home village) nostalgia is marketed through the sale of books, travel prints, and postcards. Department stores like Seibu and Mitsukoshi have capitalized on this trend by holding exhibits and craft fairs of items from rural villages around Japan. One Seibu department store in Tokyo held a "101 Japanese Village Exhibit" featuring displays, crafts, and other products sold by villagers dressed in traditional costumes. This gave shoppers the "experience" of the rural villages without ever leaving Tokyo (Creighton 1997:250).

Creighton found that department stores have other ways to attract shoppers by creating experiences that provide what she calls "edutainment" (Creighton 1994:35). As mentioned at the beginning of this chapter, education in Japan is highly prized, and admission to universities is highly competitive. Department stores have learned to cash in on the same issues that Gerber used in marketing baby foods: the well-being of the consumer's child. Department stores provide mothers with free services that make it easier for them to shop with their children, and the stores actually suggest to them that the shopping trip is important to their children. Typical department store services might include a nutrition specialist, consultations with physicians, and a lending library of books on childcare. Some stores, like Seibu, even include an indoor kids' theme park similar to Sesame Place in the United States. In fact a Sesame Place opened in Tokyo in 1990. These theme parks are marketed as providing an educational experience for children.

John F. Sherry and Robert Kozinets have studied other venues where experience is consumed. They looked at "brand stores," which are owned by a brand's manufacturer, sell only that brand, and serve to further advertise the brand to consumers. In particular they have been interested in "themed entertainment brand stores" in which the brand manufacturer is selling an experience that reinforces the brand in the consumer's eyes. Planet Hollywood and the Hard Rock Cafe as well as the World of Coca-Cola Museums in Atlanta and Las Vegas are examples. Sherry, Kozinets, and their colleagues looked closely at ESPN Zone Chicago, which was a 35,000 square foot retail space owned and operated by Walt Disney Corporation to promote its ESPN television network. While ESPN Zone shut its doors in 2010, Sherry and Kozinets' work still provides an apt example of using anthropological techniques.

Sherry, Kozinets, and their colleagues spent four months as participant observers and conducted interviews with management, staff, and customers of ESPN Zone. They documented their data through notes, audiotapes, and photographs and worked with some 500 informants. The research team consisted of three males and three females ranging in age from early 20s to late 40s. Their differing life experiences and personalities (gender, age, jock, techie) broadened the types of people they were able to interview. The team met weekly in strategy meetings where they discussed emerging themes in the research and analyzed them. They found that their differing life experiences caused them to interpret the data differently. Thus, their final analysis was richer and more complex than it would have been with a single researcher. They were interested in why people came to ESPN Zone and what their impressions of it were. The following are examples of interviewees' comments (Sherry et al. 2001):

> "I come here to watch the games. I first come to eat, and then I come to watch. It's a way to escape, release tension . . . to have fun. The major reason is I like sports. I bring my clients and vendors. There's something to capture anyone's attention."
> —"Thomas," male, early thirties, African American,
> computer network consultant (p. 466)

> "The place makes me feel different . . . Chuck E. Cheese. It's like I'm in a grown up Chuck E. Cheese. I feel uninhibited, free, and not so much concerned about things going on around."
> —"Veronica," female, Caucasian, late twenties (p. 466)

> Tonya: "I like the fact that the downstairs restaurant is set up like a studio. I mean, who doesn't want to sit in Kirk Herbstreit's [ESPN

college football sportscaster] chair? I can pretend that I am Stuart Scott or, like, the Anna Kournikova of sportscasting."

Interviewer: "So when you sit there, you become the center of attention, or at least other people notice you are there?"

Tonya: "I guess I don't really care about the other people. It's just like people that go to places to feel more connected. Like Star Wars fans, or something." (p. 483)

In true Disney fashion, employees at ESPN Zone Chicago were called "cast members" and customers were "guests." The building included restaurants and gift shops with a sports theme. There were also many opportunities to play games and participate in sports activities that included virtual car racing and snow boarding; real games, like miniature bowling; and virtual/real games like soccer in which the guest kicks a real ball toward a goal tended by a virtual goaltender. There were also elaborate rooms for viewing ESPN sports events. The most elaborate contained a 16' x 12' screen surrounded by twelve 37-inch monitors with a scrolling message screen of ESPN advertising and sports news across the top.

Sherry, Kozinets, and colleagues (2001:502, 505) suggest that Disney was selling an "experience" at ESPN Zone Chicago. "Retail theater," like ESPN Chicago, demands "a mixture of scripted role-playing and improvisation to feel authentic. . . . Consumers at ESPN Zone are experiencing being-in-the-television concurrently with being-in-the-[particular]-sportsworld and being-in-the-building. This simultaneous sensation contributes to the altered state of being-in-the-zone."

The Cultural Context of Emotion

As mentioned previously, the executives at Coca-Cola learned that consumers' emotional ties to the original Coke product played a role in their rejection of New Coke (Food Inc. 2009). This leads to the question: What role does emotion play in brand loyalty? Patricia Sunderland and Rita Denny (2007:139–170) describe the importance of a cultural analysis of emotion in consumer research. They wanted to move beyond the simplistic idea of customers' "love" of a brand and learn more about the different facets of emotion. Sunderland and Denny's interest in emotion was sparked when in a 2003 study they asked teens to keep all their candy wrappers for ten days and to write on each the location where they were purchased, what the teens were doing and with whom at the time, and their mood (Sunderland and Denny 2007:139). The predominant mood of the teens turned out to be—boredom. Sunderland and Denny expected this but were surprised at the numerous times and varied circumstances when the teens were bored. Is boredom an emotion? If so, what does this signify?

Subsequently, in 2006 when they had the chance to partner with a New Zealand advertizing agency interested in emotional appeals, they did so. Together they sought to study the sociocultural expression of emotion in advertizing among young adults in London, New York City, and Auckland in order to understand how emotion was culturally constituted. They studied six young adults (aged 18–24) in each city. First, the teens were asked to keep a diary about three emotional states in their daily life and explain in photographs and notes what these emotions looked like and felt like. Second, they were asked to bring in examples of these emotions from magazines, websites, and ads. They were told they could invite a friend to be involved in the project as well. Third, the researchers interviewed the young people about their diaries and choices of ads and showed them ads as well.

The researchers found informative cultural differences in the way the three groups viewed emotions. For the Londoners, in many examples, the emotions resulted from external events, not internal ones. One young man experienced "paranoia" (his word) when he thought the manager at the restaurant where he worked was watching him at the cash register and suspected him of stealing. Another of the Londoners described how being with miserable people could make you feel miserable. In these and other examples, the external events caused the emotion. Additionally, for the Londoners, emotions could be expressed with close friends and family but not in more public contexts.

By contrast, in New York City "stress" was described as an emotion in the diaries of the young adults. They made comments such as, "Stress feels like nothing can go right. I have no time to do anything that needs to be done." The trigger for this "emotion" was internal; it was the pressure the young adults were putting on themselves to use their time wisely and make the most of their future. Stress was about making the most of yourself. For the New Yorkers, public expressions of emotion were understandable.

The Aucklanders, on the other hand, wrote about "being strong" and "being open," two emotional states in tension. To be strong was to be composed as one prepared to take the next big wave on your surfboard or to block a goal while playing a sport. Being open is to express emotion as you feel it and tell things as they are.

Sunderland and Denny showed the same ads to the three groups of young adults and received differing responses. In one set of ads, a young man with dreadlocks is shown with his eyes closed and his head back. His hair is flying around his face as if he were shaking his head forcefully. The New York subjects thought this young man might be at a party and was in a happy state that they would like to experience. The Auckland group saw the young man as exhibiting true, strong emotions, and great passion and, similar to the New Yorkers, saw this as positive. By contrast, the London group thought the image was false or

fake or that the individual was on a drug-induced high since no one in
a normal state would behave so emotionally in public. Thus, the kinds
of feelings the three groups categorized as emotion varied as did the
source of emotion—internal for the New York and Auckland groups and
external for the London group. In addition, they responded to the same
ads in different ways. All of this suggests the existence of a cultural
context of emotion and the need to understand the nuances of this context in understanding consumer behavior.

Localization in Globalization

You can buy a Coke just about anywhere in the world. Coke is an
example of a globalized product, but it demonstrates not only the globalization of consumer goods but also their localization. In his work for
The Coca-Cola Company, Daniel Miller learned that in Trinidad, you
must understand Trini consumption patterns and the importance of
black sweet drinks and red sweet drinks in order to understand the
success of Coke.

The Coca-Cola Company is a global company that operates internationally through franchising. This means that it agrees to sell Coke con-
centrate to a local bottling plant and the plant then has the exclusive
right to sell Coke in its local region. Coke came to Trinidad in 1939, and
in 1941 US troops arrived when Britain leased military bases in Trinidad
to the United States. Thus, Coke and a US presence arrived in Trinidad
at almost the same time. The reaction to the US presence was mixed, but
somehow out of the mix of Trini and American culture, an important
drink was born—rum and Coke. While this combination became popular
stateside, it may have been even more popular in Trinidad, and it made
Coke a Trini national drink. While Coke was an imported drink, rum was
an important local drink that represented Trinidad. Rum and Coke
became a national drink rivaled only by the local beer.

While the company that originally bought the franchise and bot-
tled Coke in Trinidad was an old firm from Trinidad's days as a British
colony, it was still considered a Trinidadian company and thus local.
Equally important is that in Trinidad, Coke is a "sweet drink," not a
"soft drink." "Sweet drinks" are Trinidadian necessities of everyday
consumption. Furthermore, sweet drinks are conceptualized as either
red sweet drinks, identified with the Indian population of Trinidad, or
black sweet drinks, identified with the African population, the dominant population. Although both populations drink both types of sweet
drinks and see both as Trinidadian, Coke is locally seen as a black
sweet drink. Because sweet drinks, which have a high sugar content,
are considered necessary food items in Trinidad, the fixation back in
North America with health foods and corresponding reduction of sugar
in soft drinks would not play well in Trinidad. In fact drinks introduced
in Trinidad with low sugar content do not sell well. So the success or

failure of Coke, a product consumed globally, is best understood in local contexts, suggesting, as Miller believes, that globalization does not mean homogenization, as products sold globally have differing local meanings around the world (Miller 1998). Miller therefore disagrees with those who suggest Coke is an example of global homogenization.

Millie Creighton describes another interesting case of globalization. She explains how the Western observance of Valentine's Day became popular in Japan. Valentine's Day was introduced to Japan in 1958 by an executive of the Mary Chocolate Company, a Japanese company whose founder chose to give the company an English name. The chief executive had been in the West on Valentine's Day and decided that his company would more effectively sell its product if this day were observed in Japan. In Japan, on Valentine's Day women give gifts of chocolate to men, but men do not give gifts of any kind to women. This arrangement, which seems odd from a Western point of view, resulted from a translation mistake. Today, Valentine's Day is big business in Japan, and 10 percent of the chocolate companies' annual sales occur in February. Creighton comments that the Mary Chocolate Company's success with Valentine's Day is similar to the success of DeBeers, a Dutch diamond company that succeeded at making diamonds a symbol of love in Europe.

Since 1979, other companies in Japan have helped institute the observance of another special day. White Day is a day when men give presents that are white in color (white chocolate or vanilla biscuits, for example) to women. Like Valentine's Day, White Day is seen as connected with the West, even though it is not celebrated in the West; White Day, after all, has an English title. Valentine's Day and White Day are days when individuals give gifts to other individuals, whereas the more traditional gift-giving days in Japan involve community, not individuality. Valentine's Day is also seen as a sign of women's liberation in Japan as women are free to give as they choose, with no expected cultural constraints. However, it has become customary for women to give gifts of chocolate to their male superiors at work, as well as to the man with whom they are romantically involved, on Valentine's Day.

The custom of giving to superiors is part of traditional gift-giving holidays in Japan as well. There, gift giving reflects hierarchy; subordinates give to superiors. This aspect of traditional gift giving has crept into Valentine's Day. Creighton also suggests that there is a symbolic meaning of sweets and chocolate that reflects the dependent and inferior position of women in Japanese society. The Japanese words for *sweet* (*amai*) and for *dependence* (*amae*) come from the same linguistic root. Others have suggested that the Japanese associate alcohol with men and sweets with women and children (Creighton 1993; Edwards 1987:51–78). As in the case of Coca-Cola in Trinidad, Valentine's Day has been re-created in a local context in Japan.

Changing Values of Consumers:
Consumption in the Larger Economic Context

While the studies of emotion and young people in New York City, London, and Auckland, of Coke in Trinidad, and of Valentine's Day in Japan exemplify the importance of the cultural context of consumption, other research describes the impact of the larger economic context. How did the US economic downturn of 2008 alter consumer behavior? Timothy Malefyt (2009) and other anthropologists at BBDO (a worldwide advertising agency) determined that it changed the meaning of consumption. To learn this they conducted three ethnographic studies in 2008 and 2009 about how people had adjusted their spending as a result of the economic crisis. They conducted 72 interviews with middle-income individuals, couples, and families in the cities of Atlanta, Detroit, Charlotte, Minneapolis, and San Francisco. The interviewees were ethnically diverse and ranged in age from 21–60. The researchers interviewed them in their homes, shopped with them both online and in stores, and recorded their narratives about shopping. As Malefyt explains, narratives "guide us both 'living through' and 'thinking back' to make sense of what we do, as well as 'wishing forward' to establish goals and models for future experience" (2009:211).

By using the ethnographic methods described above, the researchers were able to document a change in their subjects' consumption patterns and the accompanying values. What they learned was that the former narrative of shopping before the 2008 downturn was one of "personal fulfillment" and "instant gratification," which was no longer valued in 2009. Instead of personal fulfillment and instant gratification, shoppers were delaying personal purchases in favor of "important" purchases for family or friends and were placing value on this new pattern. Shoppers told narratives about "'being smarter with their money,' planning out purchases ahead of time, using coupons, making lists and organizing shopping trips" (209:212). Consumers had created new values; their values had shifted from prizing the spur-of-the-moment purchase and shopping as an entertainment experience to pride in using money wisely and caring for one's family. The new values are exemplified in the following excerpt from an interview with Donna, a 38-year-old of Italian descent, married with two small children and living in a New Jersey suburb:

> "Before, if my husband or I wanted something we used to just go out and get it. I'd say, 'I'm going shopping,' not with a purpose in mind, but just to go shopping. . . . So, now we think about it and spend on what's really important, like for my children, for their education. It's helped me to be more cautious." (Malefyt 2009:213)

Additionally, Malefyt and the others found their interviewees telling stories celebrating "the deal" wherein they described purchasing their desired object for a good price:

> "Getting a deal makes me want to tell others. Like the time I got a
> $100 Donna Karan purse for $29. I kept watching it at Marshall's,
> and hung it at the back of the rack, and waited until it came down.
> I kept returning and putting it back in the back, and one day they
> reduced the price." (2009:215)

Narratives like these reveal consumers reframing former notions of "stinginess" into pride at their own resourcefulness. The behavior was seen as a valued strategy for survival in difficult economic times. While Malefyt and the others cannot predict how consumption patterns will change should the economy improve, their work documents "how spending wisely and saving money are shared competencies that promote a feeling of community-in-action. Restricted money and careful spending, rather than discouraging people not to enjoy shopping, appears to bring together feeling of community, joy and of shopping that work towards a greater good" (2009:219).

My students and I recorded a similar concern for careful, money-saving strategies, rather than easy gratification, in a study of car purchasing behavior we conducted in 2009 (Jordan, Briody et al 2009). In asking interviewees what factors determined their choice of car brand and model in their last car purchase and what factors would determine their choice in the future, we learned that low purchase cost, fuel efficiency, and low repair costs were significantly more important considerations for future purchasing decisions than they had been for the previous one. Consumers in the economic downturn found new ways to create value in the shopping experience.

CONCLUSION

Anthropologists' valuable methods and theoretical perspectives contribute to the fields of marketing and consumer behavior by providing an understanding of the interface of contested, overlapping, and intertwined cultural groupings; of consumption as action that voices acceptance and resistance; of the global as re-created in the local, and other cross-cultural similarities and differences in consumption; of identity as it is negotiated through consumptive practices; of the consumption of experience; and of the contextual nature of consumption. In addition, the anthropologists writing in this area contribute to the whole of anthropological research through their focus on the social life of commodities and on modes of consumption, a focus equally as important as the focus on modes of production.

Chapter Seven

Design Anthropology

---

*Listening to scientists and
videotaping kids at breakfast . . .*

Intel was interested in how computers were being used in extreme situations. They asked John Sherry to find out. His search for the answer led him to the Alaskan salmon industry, where he found a "tender" (the individual who acquires the catch from the fishers and transports it to the cannery) who had duct-taped a notebook computer to the wall of his ship. There the tender made entries keeping track of payments and reports vital to his business exchanges. In that environment with fish, blood, and scales everywhere, Sherry was told, "I need a computer that's so durable I can blast it with a deck hose and it will still work." Sherry returned to inform Intel that they needed to think about designing computers for rugged use. Some users need a computer that can withstand being hosed down on the deck of a ship!

In another instance, a computer company wanted to know if the packaging for its computers could be improved. They wanted to know if people who tend to be intimidated by learning how to work new computers were being put off by the difficulties of getting into the packaging before they ever plugged in the machine. To find out, an anthropologist set up a booth at a consumer trade show and asked people to volunteer to unpackage new machines in return for a small compensation. She videotaped the process and as a result learned how her company could create more consumer friendly packaging (Weise 1999).

WHY DESIGN FIRMS HIRE ANTHROPOLOGISTS

Anthropologists get close to their subject of study—in this case the potential user of a product—to get a precise idea of what end users want. "Traditional market research tools are limited by their question-and-answer format. . . . In the case of surveys, you're telling the respondent how to answer, and you're not giving them any room for anything else," explained Andrea Saveri (cited in Weise 1999:4d), who employed ethnographers at the Institute for the Future in Menlo Park, California. Ethnographers can move past that. Lucy Suchman says that as an anthropologist studying user behavior, she studies *situated action*. This means that she observes action as it is taking place. A person's next action is determined to some extent by the actions that immediately precede it. Suchman uses this level of detail in understanding human interaction with machines because she feels these are instances in which one must observe a sequence of behavior in order to understand the significance of a specific behavior (Suchman 1987). As Katherine Burr, an anthropologist who is chairman of Hanseatic Group, Inc., a quantitative fund management company that uses pattern recognition to trade securities, futures, and currencies for global institutional investors (http://www.lojagroup.com/about-loja/katherine-harvey-burr/), succinctly stated: "Preconceptions can kill you" (cited in Weise 1999:4d). Anthropologists, because their research techniques are honed for and in those situations in which they do not know enough to be able to form preconceptions, know how to research a topic with fewer preconceptions. Their formula? Go to the people; ask and watch.

In the field of product design and development, an anthropologist may be involved in creating new products (bathroom cleaners or small cooking appliances), services (packaged tours), or policies (rules for frequent shopper discounts). According to the Industrial Designers Society of America, the design field "envision(s) and give(s) shape to new, or modified, products and services" (Wasson 2000:377). As Denny explains, frequently the client is asking the anthropologist to discover "unmet needs." Denny believes that the assumption underlying this request is that the consumer is a passive vessel waiting to receive new products. As anthropologists, we know that the relationship between consumers and the products they use is more complex than this. For example, when a client asked, "What are the unmet needs in spray 'trigger' cleansers?" Denny (2002:156–157) knew to reframe the question into "What does 'clean' mean today?" Or, in response to "How is technology integrated in the home?" she knew to think in terms of questions like "What is a telephone?" "What is a television?" and "What is 'home' today?" One of the values of the anthropological perspective is the ability to step back and look at the issues being addressed in a larger context, which gets at the cultural assumptions of the original question and leads to a more holistic and valuable answer. Meeting the consumers' unmet needs is a complex problem, as consumers frequently cannot articulate those needs and do not realize what might be useful to them (Wasson 2000:377). Before they became available, I had no idea I needed either Velcro fasteners or a gourmet coffee shop on every corner.

Ethnographic techniques have become popular in the design field because they fill a void. At one time, designers depended primarily on human factors research, which developed out of cognitive psychology and marketing research. Human factors research takes into account human cognitive abilities and the things that make a product easy for humans to use; for example, if the hardware on a door that you must push to open is flat, it becomes obvious to the user that to open the door she must push, not pull (Wasson 2000). While human factors research is useful for understanding the best way to design some products, for others, it is too abstract and removed from everyday reality because it is often conducted in controlled environments, like labs (Van Veggel n.d.). In addition, this type of research focuses on what goes on in individuals' heads and does not take into account the social and cultural context and group interaction. Thus, there is no opportunity to observe and learn from the rich interaction of social beings in which products are not only used but also understood. Anthropologists are the social scientists uniquely situated by training to analyze that rich social milieu and that group-patterned interaction.

Other information-gathering techniques, such as user surveys, focus groups, demographic studies, and product sales history, come from sociology and its use of quantitative methods. These techniques provide useful information, but they depend on past history and what the user tells the researcher. Again, the data they provide are not as rich as the data that ethnography can provide. They do not get the researcher out there, watching the user in action (Wasson 2000:377–378). Data that are self-reported inform the researcher about the attitudes and perceptions of the individual but do not show the researcher how a person actually uses the product. For all of us, what we say we do and what we actually do are two very different things. Through participant observation, either real or virtual (video), the anthropologist learns about what people actually do, which in turn indicates whether the design of the product facilitates its use. In surveys and focus groups, the subjects of a study are limited to answering the questions the researchers pose; the subjects do not create the questions themselves. As discussed in chapter 3 on methods, one of the contributions of anthropological techniques is that they allow the subjects to tell the researchers the questions that they need to ask (Van Veggel n.d.).

It is due to the limitations of the other methods that design firms are turning to anthropologists. Ethnographic techniques are not the only valuable tools anthropologists offer, however. After all, anyone can videotape consumers in the act of using a product. In addition, anthropologists offer a theoretical grounding and an understanding of the interrelationships of the variables that are essential to providing valuable and useful analysis of the data. As Wasson (2002:25) puts it, "a videotape alone cannot answer questions about how, for instance, particular user-product interactions are situated in consumers' family dynamics, work pressures, and cultural beliefs."

ANTHROPOLOGICAL RESEARCH IN PRODUCT DESIGN

Whether called in to help develop a new product, what Susan Squires (2002) calls "discovery" research, or called in to help improve an existing product, the anthropologist is likely to work closely with the designers who actually create the product.

Discovery Research: Developing New Products

In a discovery project, Squires worked for a large breakfast food company interested in creating a new breakfast food for kids. Squires was hired to find out about family breakfast routines and to learn what kids ate. She and her colleagues formed two, two-member teams. Each team had one social scientist and one designer. They familiarized themselves with market research and industry reports on breakfast food consumption, as these are often sources of information about what is considered "acceptable" thinking on breakfast food. Then, Squires and her colleagues recruited families to participate in their study. The Kelly family, for instance, was recruited because the mother had participated in an earlier study for the same client on what people say about breakfast and breakfast food. Squires and her colleagues wanted to see if breakfast activities actually matched what people said. So the teams arrived at homes at 6:30 A.M. with video cameras, tape recorders, pens, and paper to record the early morning routines of families. They came with a long list of questions they hoped to answer (Squires 2002:110):

What were the morning routines at the Kelly house? Who was there and who was not?

What other foods might be available?

What is it like to coax a four-year-old to eat at 6:30 in the morning?

What else had to get done before the family departed the house?

Where did the family go after leaving the house?

Did anyone pick up food after leaving the house?

After taping the morning's activities, they returned to their office to review the tapes and transcripts and determine their next step. They wanted to understand breakfast in the context of the Kelly family's lives, so they followed family members in the following days. They observed the kids at day care and contacted the father at work.

Squires and her colleagues continued to follow families until they could identify a pattern of breakfast behavior relevant to their client's concerns. They found that moms were interested in nutrition and kids were interested in fun. In addition, kids (and frequently even parents) were not eating breakfast at home before leaving for the day. The reason for this was simple: the time was too early in the day. Modern North American families begin their day at 6:30 and 7:00 A.M., a time so early that their bodies are not yet hungry. Young children are ignoring Mom's nutritious breakfast and are either not eating or finding something more fun to eat, like a heavily sugared cereal that turns the milk blue. This lack of breakfast frequently results in kids getting hungry mid-morning. One four-year-old whom Squires videotaped ate his lunch during the 10:00 A.M. recess at the day-care center he attended. His body was not hungry at 6:30 but was by 10:00. Squires's (2002) findings helped the breakfast manufacturer create a new breakfast food (Go-Gurt) for kids that is fun and portable; it is yogurt in a tube.

In another discovery project, Heiko Sacher (2002) was involved in designing an Internet software package for scientists. The design project was conducted by a team composed of members from the software company that was the client and members, including Sacher, from GVO, a California design firm. The team consisted of two social scientists, one designer, and two software developers. Their task was to create a user interface for a database containing over four million items; the project lasted three months. The existing user interface for the software worked the way surfing the Web works, but the users, lab research scientists, were evaluating it with comments like "it doesn't seem efficient," "it is clumsy," "I don't like it—don't ask me why" (Sacher 2002:188–189). So the team listened to the scientists describe how they go about gathering data in their research. The scientists used expressions like "go there," and "find" or "discover," and "get" or "pull out," and "put together," "collate," and "understand." The following are examples of their comments.

> "I go to the database X and I go to database Z and I read about it there." "I wanna know what's out there, what others have done."

> "I take the hits from the search . . . pick a few . . . go back and look at those analysis results . . . then from there I might take those and search again . . . then I'll get the items themselves and take that . . ." (Sacher 2002:189)

Sacher and his team realized that the scientists' mental model for doing research is different from the pattern one uses in surfing the Web. Scientists go out from the home base, gather data, and bring it back to compare and collate. Then they go out again, gather more data, bring it back, keep the good, and throw out the rest. In contrast, in a Web search, you enter a search topic and are taken through a string of sites, creating a maze of interconnections. An Internet research package designed on this typical Web surfing model would not be used by scientists whose lab research techniques follow the model described above. Consequently, the software had to be designed to work the way the scientists work. Analysis of language used by scientists describing their own research endeavors and the difficulties they experienced finding things on the Internet led Sacher to the clues that helped him develop a successful software package for scientists.

Christina Wasson describes work for Steelcase done at E-Lab, a design firm that relied heavily on anthropological techniques. Steelcase manufactures office furniture and office partitions. Frequently an office is structurally one large space that is then divided by partitions into offices and work cubicles. The designers working at Steelcase thought in terms of two types of work areas: individual—one's individual office—and group—meeting rooms. E-Lab research, however, showed them that workers were using space in ways the designers had never assumed; workers met and discussed work in areas such as hallways, not designed for group work. Consequently, Steelcase began thinking in terms of products, such as whiteboards, used for writing down ideas with markers, and chairs, which could be placed in these other communal spaces to make it easier to work there. As a result of the E-Lab study, it has now become routine at Steelcase to consider workers' needs for work-enabling products in spaces formerly considered "dead" space (Wasson 2000:384).

In projects like Steelcase, researchers collect data in numerous ways. In one project in an office setting, Wasson and her colleagues used eight stationary video cameras, which operated eight hours a day for five days. In addition during that time, three researchers were engaged full-time in interviewing, shadowing subjects, touring their desks, and in general observing, all with a handicam to capture what they saw. Employees were also asked to keep diaries of their activities related to the project. After that data collection, the researchers returned to their own office to begin the time-consuming task of viewing and analyzing their tapes and other collected data (Wasson, personal communication June 29, 2002).

Ken Anderson and Rogério de Paula (2006) of Intel provide insight into how layers of cultural difference that are often overlooked can point the way to possible new products. While studying the lives of urban women in Brazil, they stumbled upon an example of how US cor-

porations disproportionately favor Western values in designing and
developing products. This discovery came while riding on a bus and
later a boat to get to and from their research site for the project on
women. They describe a bus ride in which riders, on entering the bus,
spontaneously joined in conversations in progress so that the bus, complete with loud music in the background, was a noisy affair where multiple, simultaneous, conversations were ongoing and no passenger
could escape participation. They describe how Antonio, their guide who
attempted to sit silently and stare out the window, was reluctantly
drawn in:

> A woman in the seat next to him asks the man in front of them
> whether he would give her an ice-cream he is carrying in his cool-
> er—he is a street vendor, who probably spent the day selling ice-
> cream on the beach. They start negotiating . . . and that conversa-
> tion, as by "magic," turns into one about religious values. . . . Soon
> they, together with a woman standing, who has just joined the con-
> versation, are engaging Antonio. He looks out more. They talk more
> to him. Despite repeated attempts at resistance, soon he is pulled
> into the bus conversation. (2006:65–66)

Anderson and de Paula describe another experience that occurred on a
30-minute ferry ride to the mainland:

> [A]s soon as the boat left the island, people started moving about.
> Kids went to the back to play, girls grouped together with some
> young guys also on the back and started talking, laughing, discuss-
> ing, and the like. . . . On the rooftop, adults also had fun—some
> pulled out some beer cans from the coolers, some started singing
> and trying some samba steps in the limited space they had. . . . Ev-
> eryone was drawn into this single collectivism. (2006:68).

By contrast, when crowded into temporary, public, transportation
vehicles, whether bus, subway, or train, people in the US tend to practice "being together alone" (2006:68). This means they may practice
"cocooning" in which they create a place of individual solitude while
among the masses. My students recently observed this while conducting a field project on city buses in Denton, Texas. Most other students
on the bus had settled down in their seats with earphones in their ears
listening to their MP3 players. None were interacting but instead had
created a bubble of individual solitude. This is cocooning. The other
common practice in the US is the "absent present" where the individual
is socially engaged, but not with his bus mates. Rather, he is chatting
on his cell phone or texting. Anderson and de Paula explain that Intel
and other technology companies are focused on making products that
fit these documented trends in the West, meaning "the trends of social
isolation, escapism and a focus on 'me'"(2006:70). In so doing, however,
they are missing the opportunity to capitalize on—that is, creating

products geared to—other cultural realities as exemplified by the extemporaneous social collectiveness occurring on public transportation in Brazil.

Furthermore, Anderson and de Paula suggest that developing products for the unique Brazil experience would allow Intel and others to avoid the accusation of colonization in a postcolonial era. This accusation has been leveled at multinational corporations for introducing the products valued in the West into other cultural contexts and creating need where previously it did not culturally exist. Today, we are beginning to see new products develop that serve the social need exemplified in the Brazilian boat ride. Game applications for smart phones effectively turn the phone into a game board and allow co-located friends to play a game together passing the phone-as-game board back and forth among themselves.

Problems with Internet privacy provide another example of a possible new product need according to Martin Ortlieb, an anthropologist at Google. Based on interviews over a two-year period in Germany, Switzerland, the UK, and the US, he concluded that Internet users were asking themselves two questions: (1) "How should one behave and interact on the Web?" (2) "What kind of behavior can one expect from one's partners in the online communication/interaction/ transaction spaces from Social Networking to Online auctions and from Email and instant messaging to blogs and reviews?" (2011:311). Users were not sure what the etiquette should be in their own behavior and what the guidelines should be for situations that cross over from online to off-line communication. They were fearful that they could not trust the strategies they use to protect their online transactions or space. Ortlieb learned just how much fear there was about the Internet and privacy.

He determined that part of the issue came down to how online relationships are structured. The predominant model is one of "concentric circles of social distance" in which private, family, friends, and public are typical levels of protection built into Internet sites. These simple levels do not express the intricacies of user experience on the Web. Ortlieb listed six work-arounds users were putting into practice to give themselves more control:

1. ***Lock-down, Restriction, Withdrawal.*** Short of not using the Internet at all, Ortlieb found that users limited their use. For example, they might put their Facebook profile on the most restrictive settings or not use Facebook at all.

2. ***Splitting Your ID.*** Users tried to compartmentalize their Web-life by using different e-mail addresses for different purposes, for example one e-mail for eBay, one for family, one for newsletters and subscriptions.

3. *Separating Domains.* Users made an effort to keep their off-line life far from their online life by, for example, picking up eBay purchases in a parking lot or having them mailed to a P.O. Box.

4. *Manual Individual Control.* Users manually tried to prevent problems by deleting their browser history each time they closed the browser or searching the Terms and Conditions in any Internet site contract for possible hidden charges and downloading these contracts into a Word document before agreeing to them.

5. *Hope.* Ortlieb detected a true note of anxiety among users regarding password protection. All commented on the difficulty of remembering many passwords and provided examples of how they managed this password proliferation problem, for example always using the same password or keeping a password list on their computer. They were aware, however, of the dangers of their lax password habits. In focus groups, they even exchanged ideas with each other on how to improve their password safety. Lacking a good solution, users fell back on *hope*, the hope that their poor password protection habits would not lead to their passwords being detected by hackers.

6. *Different Measures for the World than for Me.* Throughout the research, Ortlieb noticed that users expressed dismay at the inappropriate Internet behavior they feared from others on the Internet while doing some of these same behaviors themselves. This included reading their ex's e-mail entries or surfing to find out personal information about others that could cause them problems (2011:314–317).

Ortlieb concluded that his research uncovered a need designers should tackle. The concentric circles of private, family, friends, and public were too simplistic, and users would welcome more nuanced approaches to controlling access to their information online. The issues of identity protection and confidential information were too complex for the current methods websites were using.

Redesigning Old Products

The importance of observing human behavior is underscored in Lucy Suchman's study of human–machine interaction (Suchman 1987). Suchman begins by looking at what may seem an unlikely group of humans in an unlikely place: she looks at sailors on the high seas. Tapping previous anthropological research, she describes Thomas Gladwin's (1964) work comparing Trukese navigation of the open seas with European navigation of the open seas. Europeans take to the seas with a charted "course," a plan, which they use to determine their every move. If forced "off course," they first alter the plan to remedy the situation and then strive to follow the alteration to get "back on course." They attempt at every turn to stay "on course." The Trukese, by contrast, never set a course. They have an objective, a place they eventually wish to end up. To get there they respond to situations as they arise and consider wind, waves, fauna, stars, and the sound of the water on the side of the boat in determining any "next move." There is never a plan for reaching this end destination; decisions are made as they are needed. At any point in time, the Trukese navigator could tell you his objective, the place he wishes to reach, but not his plan, the course he will follow to get there. Suchman suggests that the European and Trukese navigators represent two different views of human-directed action and that more frequently than we realize we operate in the Trukese fashion. To understand human–machine interaction, one can look at Trukese-type behavior.

In working to develop more helpful instructions for the operation of copy machines, Suchman videotaped pairs of machine users attempting a complicated copying task. To complete the task, users were required to turn to the machine's "expert help system," a computer-based system in which the copier displayed instructions for humans to follow in completing copying tasks. The expert help system of the copy machine had been developed under the assumption that the humans using it were working through a plan in the same manner that European navigators follow a charted course. However, by observing the ways in which humans in real situations figured out what action to take next in interacting with the copy machine, Suchman found they operated more like the Trukese. They based the next step on what they had learned from their last action, not necessarily on what the expert help system prescribed. Her detailed analysis of human–machine interaction demonstrated some of the problems humans encountered when trying to follow the expert help system and why it is so difficult to create one that is foolproof. This allowed for better expert help systems to be developed.

Evaluating Existing Products

A related area of research to product design is product evaluation. Squires was asked by a large international firm to evaluate the usefulness of desktop conferencing equipment for its Information System Services Division. She did so by testing the usefulness of two types of desktop conferencing equipment. In one case, individuals in diverse locations could use a whiteboard (software that lets you collaborate in real time with others via graphic information) on their computers to communicate ideas during a conference. In the second, a video camera was added to this situation so that they could not only communicate with each other but also see each other as well. Squires set up simulation rooms and asked employees in the division to try the equipment.

She observed pairs located in separate rooms interacting through the equipment. She also conducted focus groups and online surveys. The majority of participants said they thought the video conferencing equipment was the best and was useful; yet she observed that, when using it, many of them turned off the video portion of the equipment within the first ten minutes of the conference. Employees assumed they would use the video component but, in actuality, they did not use it. In this study the observation phase proved vital. Relying on the focus groups and surveys alone, Squires would have concluded that video conferencing worked well. It was the observation that provided her with evidence to the contrary. On learning these results, the company decided to delay the purchase of expensive desktop conferencing equipment altogether (Squires 2002).

Alice Peinado, Magdalena Jarvin, and Juliette Damoisel (2011) worked on a collaborative project with designers and executives from three banks and two insurance companies to develop a new methodology for designing bank and insurance products for customers in France. Most of the bankers and insurance executives came from a computer engineering background and used quantitative research where customers were segmented according to age and socioeconomic background, and products were developed for specific segments. They were confounded by what appeared to be irrational choices by their customers. Peinado and her colleagues convinced the bankers and insurance executives that if they wanted an innovative, design-centered approach, they would do well to use qualitative research that would put them in touch with the real users of their products, not just statistical segments. The anthropologists hoped to show how those irrational choices were the result of specific life choices respective to unique and individual life stories.

The anthropologists decided to interview "clients," focusing on two areas of questioning: (1) "What is money, what associations does it give rise to—happiness/anguish; richness/poverty; openness/closeness?" and (2) "How does the representation of money evolve during life and according to life's events—live with/without; earn/lose; primary/secondary place" (Peinado, et al. 2011:262). They interviewed 18 individuals ranging in age from 15 to 80 with differing life situations and socioeconomic backgrounds, none of whom were actual clients of the banks or insurance companies involved in the research. The interviews were videotaped. Additionally they observed daily happenings in three banks and one insurance agency for one working day each and talked with employees about their jobs. After the anthropological interviews were finished, the designers gave the interviewees a booklet for them to note, in words or images (drawings or collages), further thoughts about money and about their relationship with banks and insurance companies.

The findings were a surprise to the bankers and insurance executives. The anthropologists found that there were multiple variables that determined the interviewee's perception of money and relationship to banks and insurance companies. No one variable determined their thinking nor did age or socioeconomic level; the interviewees, however, repeatedly brought up trust, face-to-face interaction, and ethics. They questioned the role of banks and insurance companies in society. (The research was conducted in 2010 during the ongoing financial crisis.)

The interviews with the bank workers were informative. The bank workers explained that their customers wanted personal counseling, while the bank's hierarchy demanded sales. The bank workers had to juggle both. Customers wanted a banker who knew them well and could give advice based on their specific situations; the bank employees, on the other hand, were trying to meet sales targets they felt were unrealistic, and they knew that offering the wrong product to a customer could end the trust relationship. To top this off, the customers' individual situations were different and required unique sets of financial products. Customers could spot the banker who tried to sell them the products of the day rather than the products that suited them.

To help the bankers and insurance executives relate to these actual life situations, the anthropologists used video clips of "real people" from the interviews. Ultimately, the designers designed an interactive-based interface that allowed "clients to personalize their bank and insurance information, assess their overall financial situation, simulate future actions, and dialogue directly with their banks and insurances" (Peinado et al. 2011:271). Since the banks and insurance companies were actually all competitors, no new products were developed as part of this project. Instead, the deliverables were the methodology itself, the knowledge from the research and the interactive, Internet, interface tool.

CONCLUSION

The anthropologist is the new kid on the block in design firms. While anthropologists' skills have been recognized only recently as valuable in this field, designers have been quick to appreciate their usefulness. Just as in the fields of marketing and consumer behavior, anthropologists' ability to get close to the consumer, to let the consumer formulate the questions, and to see the rich, contextual issues surrounding product use is an ability that makes important contributions to design research.

Chapter Eight

Organizational Anthropology

It's not just about business anymore . . .

In the introduction to this text, I explained that "business anthropology" is, to some degree, a misnomer for the field I am describing, because the "field," as I construe it and as anthropologists practice it, is not limited to work in for-profit businesses. This is nowhere more the case than in the area of organizational anthropology—the study of complex organizations from an anthropological perspective. In the 1930s and 1940s this field was referred to as "industrial anthropology," just as the corresponding field in psychology was "industrial psychology." Today, however, since industry makes up fewer of the business organizations social scientists study and service organizations make up more, the field has been renamed "organizational anthropology." While the term organizational anthropology was coined to cover work in business organizations, in the last decade it has become clear that organizational anthropology is not just about business anymore. Its subject matter has become broader to include all manner of complex organizations.

THE TYPES OF ORGANIZATIONS ANTHROPOLOGISTS STUDY

While the missions of complex organizations may differ, a recent review of organizational anthropology shows that complex organizations face similar problems in managing employees and work processes

100

and in fulfilling their respective missions whether they are corporations, hospitals, or schools. Anthropologists are working in a variety of organization types (Caulkins and Jordan 2013). I begin with a review of some of these organizations and of the work anthropologists are doing.

Of course, we still work in the for-profit sector. In addition to *large corporations*, some anthropologists study *small- and medium-sized businesses*. Doug Caulkins (1998) worked with small- and medium-sized businesses in Mid Wales to answer the question: Why does a manager from one part of the country have difficulty managing a plant in another part of the country? He learned that the answer was culture. Even though Wales is part of England, Welsh values are different from English values, and businesses in Mid Wales that are managed according to English values rather than Welsh values do not flourish. For example, at ABCTech, where management is based on an English model of organization, the structure is hierarchical and the environment is socially uncomfortable for employees who watch the managing director fly by helicopter between his home and office. On the other hand, at three other companies, a clothing design and manufacturing firm and two high-tech firms, Welsh values prevail—the companies are family businesses in which the employees are treated like family and friends.

Some of the factors that make these companies more appealing and less hierarchical are that the owners socialize with the employees after work, whole families (father and son, husband and wife) are employed in the business, and child care is provided. Here hierarchy has been replaced with egalitarianism. In-house training at these companies means employees are picked for their interest, natural abilities, and personality and then trained in their jobs. This is not the standard English business model.

Caulkins concluded that the standard English business model, which ABCTech exemplified, promotes a pattern that is not successful in the Mid Wales region of Great Britain and that regional cultural diversity can demonstrate the usefulness of developing diverse models for businesses.

Anthropological work in organizations goes far beyond studies of for-profit organizations, however. Anthropologists have also contributed studies of *government agencies*; for example, Daniel Neyland (2013) worked with the city council in a regional city in the United Kingdom to improve success in their curbside recycling scheme, a task that included an organizational problem with the way in which data about curbside recycling were collected. Eyal Ben-Ari and Efat El-Ron (2002) studied *military organizations*, specifically a multinational peace-keeping force, and described the organizational tension such troops experience between their allegiances to their national military and to the international troops with which they are participating. In *education*, not only is each school and university an organization but so

is the school district. Edmund Hamann, Saloshna Vandeyar, and Juan
Sanchez Garcia (2013), for example, compared the organizational characteristics of schools in the United States, South Africa, and Mexico.
Other anthropologists, like Paul Durrenburger and Suzan Erem
(2013), continue the work started by William Whyte (1948), whose
study involving labor unions at Bundy Tubing was mentioned in chapter 2. Durrenburger has studied American labor unions over a period
of decades and provides an understanding of how law, policy, industrial
organization, and historical processes have shaped the organization of
unions in the US.

Both Scarlett Shaffer (2008) and Shirley Fiske (2008) provide
information on anthropologists working directly for *nonprofit organizations*, such as Care, which "tackles underlying causes of poverty so that
people can become self-sufficient" (http://www.care.org/careswork/
whatwedo/index.asp), and Heifer International, whose mission is "to
work with communities to end hunger and poverty and to care for the
Earth" (http://www.heifer.org/inside/mission). Anthropologists are well
suited for work in organizations such as these since they are good at
getting beyond bureaucratic views to an understanding of the world of
poverty from the perspective of those who live it. Nonprofit work has a
long tradition in anthropology, and much of our understanding of the
workings of nonprofits comes from anthropologists employed by them.

In addition, many university-based anthropologists work with
NGOs (nongovernmental organizations) in conducting their fieldwork,
and frequently their fieldwork directly involves analysis of the actions
of NGOs at their field sites. Ralph Litzinger (2006), for example, analyzed the Critical Ecosystem Partnership Fund (CEPF) in China. In the
process, he learned about its relationships with its funders, such as the
World Bank and the MacArthur Foundation, as well as with the Chinese government. The varied agendas of these other organizations had
a significant impact on the functioning of CEPF. Other anthropologists
study *indigenous organizations*. Martinez Novo (2013), for example,
has studied the decline of indigenous social movement organizations in
Latin America, while Sarah Holcombe and Patrick Sullivan (2013)
focus on indigenous organizations in Australia and the ways these
organizations provide social services in remote regions.

Another area that is becoming important is our knowledge of *virtual organizations* (Wasson 2013). Among those is what Bonnie Nardi
named "placeless organizations" of which Doctors Without Borders and
the World Trade Organization are examples. These organizations have
the following characteristics: "(a) work is guided by a commitment . . .
to social transformation, (b) participants come from multiple diverse
organizations, (c) work is conducted at multiple shifting sites, (d) the
organizational structure is a hierarchy of nucleus + distributed vetted
participants, and (e) key participants are not in a traditional relation

of paid employment" (Wasson 2013; Nardi 2007:7). Wasson explains that this is an emergent organizational form that is growing in popularity. Placeless means location is not important for the organization; its activities occur in multiple places around the world (Nardi 2007:17). Although placeless organizations may be structured as a hierarchy, they are actually quite egalitarian, and the "nucleus" (a managing group) primarily plays a coordinating function. The work of the organization is conducted by the "distributed vetted participants" who are the individuals or organizations selected for membership around the world. In Doctors Without Borders, for example, the vetted participants would be the doctors themselves. The concept of placeless organizations also flies against the assumption that participants must be paid in order to dedicate large amounts of energy to carrying out the goals of an organization.

Medical anthropologists are working in *health care organizations* where they find issues similar to those found in corporations, schools, and many other types of complex organizations. Elisa Sobo and her colleagues, for example, studied the implementation of an HIV testing intervention at the Veterans Health Administration (VHA) in the US and documented the differing agendas of stakeholder groups across the implementation project. Sobo and colleagues were able to provide suggestions for improving communication across these diverse groups at the VHA (Sobo, Bowman, Aarons et al. 2008). Lack of communication and differing agendas are issues that are common in all organizations.

Many of the issues that other anthropologists are finding in schools, indigenous organizations, hospitals, and virtual organizations are the same ones I see in working with corporations. Thus, anthropologists are working across multiple organizational types and amassing a body of knowledge about how organizations work. While some anthropologists conduct these studies for research purposes, others work directly for the organization to solve its problems (Jordan and Caulkins 2013).

SOLVING PROBLEMS IN COMPLEX ORGANIZATIONS

Using Meetings to Understand Cultural Interaction

How exactly do these anthropologists conduct this work and how do they benefit the organization? An example is Elizabeth Briody's work with a large US-based corporation. In one project for them, she was asked to assist in solving problems with the implementation of a new program to develop a car seat that could be used in models of cars sold in the US and beyond (Briody 2013). The engineering groups of three different car units within the corporation were brought together to develop a model for a car seat that could be manufactured for use by all three. Previously, all three had different seats, and the corporation was interested in the savings generated by producing the same seat for three of its units. Briody was invited by the chief engineer in charge of overseeing the development of this new seat to participate in the meetings in which engineers from the three units were to decide how to construct a seat that each unit could use. In all, Briody observed 23 meetings. Since others in the meetings were taking notes, she was able to take notes as well, and she recorded the conversations as accurately as she could. She also conducted four follow-up interviews, one with the chief engineer and one with each of the engineers representing the three car units.

The meetings were contentious, and it did not appear that all three units were going to be able to agree on a common car seat. Briody identified a number of problems. One was that each unit was autonomous in the corporation and had to generate its own profit. Therefore, each engineer wanted to minimize the cost of the new seat for his unit and make sure the new seat satisfied the needs of his unit's customers. There was also a clash over different work practices—especially between Groups A and C. Group A in the US worked with its parts suppliers to be sure that all the technical specifications for parts were accurate early in the process; otherwise they would have to compensate the suppliers for any changes made later. Group C in Germany routinely made modifications in design throughout the process and did not have to specify them accurately at the beginning. They were not expected to compensate suppliers if changes were made during this modification process. This difference in work practices caused conflict as Group A was frustrated that Group C did not get its final specifications for the seat submitted at the onset. Group C could not see why this was a problem. Part of the dialogue in one meeting entailed an exchange where Group C suggested that a Group A engineer come to Germany to understand the requirements there; Group A responded that there were no plans to send a representative to Germany, indicating Group A's unwillingness to learn about the cultural differences of Group C.

As a result of uncovering these and other problems, Briody made three recommendations. The corporation should: (1) include the impact of the lengthy negotiations and slow progress on the program when weighing the costs and benefits of moving to a single seat design; (2) strengthen its commitment to converging seats (employees were paid by their home units and were consequently more loyal to the home unit than to this seat program; the corporation would need to make it clear that the seat program success would be rewarded); and (3) bring in cross-cultural trainers to help the three sides understand each other's point of view. Thus, Briody's study resulted in specific recommendations for management that would help them make better decisions about whether to undergo a program like this and how to make it work.

Enlisting Employees as Researchers

Another example comes from the work of Christopher Darrouzet, Helga Wild, and Susann Wilkinson (2009) who have worked as consultants to the Veterans Health Administration, part of US Department of Veterans Affairs, (VA). They were asked by one VA medical center to tackle its problems with the patient discharge system; it was taking too long to discharge patients after doctors had cleared them to leave the hospital. Darrouzet and his team used a process they called "participatory ethnography" in which they brought staff of the hospital into the data gathering as "paraethnographers" and put them to work "puzzling out" the complex issues that plagued the organization. Thus, staff were recruited to work alongside the researchers in conducting ethnography. Furthermore, they would be full participants in the analysis and design of recommendations for change (2009:65).

Patient discharge at the VA hospital involved first deciding if a patient was medically ready to be discharged. This was followed by a number of steps needed to make the discharge happen, including arrangements for family notification, patient transport, and continuing care after discharge (prescriptions and doctors, for example). For the hospital, the discharge process also included getting the patient ready to leave and then getting the room ready for a new patient once the current one was gone. The goal of Darrouzet's project was to understand the discharge process, find the inefficiencies and problems, and determine how these problems prevented other parts of the hospital from running smoothly. For example, failure to quickly prepare the room for new arrivals can cause a backup in admissions of new patients.

The team began with a day-long orientation and planning workshop during which the team members (consultants and hospital staff) discussed all aspects of the problem. They determined what places in the hospital to visit, what practices they needed to understand, and with whom they needed to speak. For the remainder of the day, the consultants taught the staff members how to conduct ethnography, meaning they explained to them how to observe by looking for patterns and how to engage their colleagues in conversations that would allow the staff paraethnographers to understand their colleagues' perspectives. The intent was to get the staff paraethnographers out of their own workplaces and into the workplaces of others in the hospital so that they could see the problems from new points of view.

As I explain to my clients, everyone in a large organization is sitting in his own closet with the door partially open. Each person can see only the part that is visible through his partially open door. So people make decisions about the entire organization based on their own partial view. The fact that staff members in a large, complex organization see only a partial view is not an employee's fault; it is a consequence of working in such an organization. Darrouzet and his colleagues were giving staff members of the VA hospital an opportunity to see the view of the organization through the partially opened doors of their colleagues in different departments; the paraethnographers got to sit in others' closets.

For this project, the paraethnographers talked with a wide range of staff members, including those who worked in the pharmacy and in the medical and surgical patient units, MDs still in training but who were on staff at the hospital, attending physicians, housekeeping workers responsible for room cleaning, respiratory therapists, social workers, and patient transporters. Over a three-day period, they spoke to some 50 staff members on all hospital shifts. Always it was necessary to get permission from the person being observed and interviewed and let him know his participation was voluntary, confidential, and unrelated to employee evaluations. The conversations were held in private settings away from the workplace if possible.

Periodically during each of the three days, the research staff (consultants and paraethnographers) "huddled" to discuss what they had learned so far. For example, the team learned what the view was like from the closet of the head of the pharmacy department. One of the holdups in patient discharge had been the length of time it took to get the prescriptions for take-home medications filled. The doctor writes the prescription; the pharmacist fills it, and in some cases meets with the patient to give her instructions on taking the medication. The head of the pharmacy department told the team that the doctors would have to write the prescriptions by 2:00 P.M. the previous day in order for them to be filled and ready for the patient to be discharged the following morning. The doctors complained that at 2:00 P.M. they would not even know if the patient was well enough to go home the next day. The doctors wanted the opportunity to extend the amount of time they had to submit the prescriptions. The head pharmacists explained that they could not fill prescriptions after 2:00 P.M. in time for the patient to be discharged the next morning because they did not have enough staff on the evening and night shifts to get prescriptions ready by 10:00 A.M.

At the end of this data gathering process, a two-day workshop was held for all the participants. In this workshop, all the information gathered was reviewed and recommendations for solutions to the problems were made. The team decided the best discharge time would be 11:00 A.M., as this would give the nurse time to prepare the patient for discharge, the pharmacy time to fill the prescriptions, and housekeeping the time to clean the room for the next arrival in the afternoon. To make this work, the processes throughout the hospital had to change.

Doctors' rounds were moved to 9:00 A.M. from 10:00 A.M. so that doctors would have time to write discharge paperwork. The doctors turned in prescriptions to the pharmacy by 9:00 P.M. on the night previous to discharge. The pharmacy hired more pharmacy technicians to work under the supervision of the pharmacists so that prescriptions turned in by 9:00 P.M. could be ready by the next morning. The hospital hired two more doctors to work for the hospital who could manage care delivery and work with residents and medical students. The bed control nurse began tracking when patients were slotted for discharge and when they actually left the hospital so the hospital would have data demonstrating how well the process was working, and she also chaired a new "Bed Flow" committee that met once a month to discuss issues with the new process. Six months after putting the new plans in place, average discharge time had moved up to 1:00 P.M. Previously too many patients were not discharged until after 4:00 P.M. when the discharge support staff, including most housekeeping employees tasked with preparing rooms for new patients, had already gone home for the day. While the hospital had not yet met its 11:00 A.M. goal, the improvements were substantial.

Working as an Employee in Order to Understand a Business

In 1997, Karen Ho was working at a Wall Street investment bank as prefieldwork for research on "investment banks' role in the downsizing of 'corporate America'" (2009:177) when she got downsized. Subsequently in 1998 and 1999 she undertook 17 months of fieldwork among Wall Street investment bankers during which she conducted participant observation and 100 interviews. She found that 25 years ago US public corporations were seen as stable institutions providing goods and services, responsible to both shareholders and employees, and with a long-term time frame for success through product development. Today, however, corporations' primary mission is to increase shareholder value in the short term so that what is in the best interest of the employees is no longer a concern of the corporation. Ho's research suggests that

> the organizational culture of Wall Street links the construction and experience of downsizing for investment bankers to that of many workers in corporate America and that an investment-banking model of employment and corporate culture has been writ large to serve as a disciplinary model for workplace relations and a catalyst for financial crisis. (2009:178)

Ho explains how the role of Wall Street investment banks in the merger, acquisition, and restructuring of corporations has led to measuring a corporation's success by its ability to generate short-term stock price increases. Investment bank organizational culture is characterized by booms and busts, cycles of hiring and layoffs. The constant threat of losing one's job shapes the culture of investment bankers, who, while possibly the highest paid workers in the world, have no job security. The high pay is compensation for the job instability. Much of their pay comes in the annual bonus, which is based on the revenue they generate for the bank through their work on corporate mergers, acquisitions, and other financial "deals." These deals are valued for the immediate increase in stock price; the long-term effects on the corporations involved, which may be disastrous, are not of concern. It is only the immediate short-term that counts. Ho suggests that investment bankers have realigned corporations according to this Wall Street organizational culture, which values short-term profit for shareholders and ignores the values of long-term production and growth, and responsibility to employees. Her work helps us understand the culture of Wall Street that led to the 2008 financial crisis.

Another who viewed the 2008 economic crisis and subsequent world economic problems through an anthropological lens is Jillian Tett. She is a reporter for the *Financial Times* and also an anthropologist who used her anthropological skills to understand the financial world before the 2008 crisis. In fact she had predicted much of what happened in 2008 in her prior columns.

CONCLUSION

Anthropologists are amassing a large body of knowledge about multiple types of complex organizations and are working with these organizations to improve organizational processes. In addition, anthropological research demonstrates the global nature of organizational networks. Both Briody's and Ho's work demonstrate how complex organizations of varied types are connected around the world in multiple ways. Work in organizational anthropology is not just about understanding issues internal to an organization, it is also about understanding the ways in which organizations partner and interact to impact communities, nation-states, and world economics and politics. In other words, it is also about global processes. The next chapter will address globalization directly.

Chapter Nine

Understanding Issues of Globalization

*Around the world in a
single business transaction . . .*

Today the Golden Arches of McDonald's can be seen at 33,000 restaurants where 64 million customers are served a day in 119 countries around the world (McDonald's 2012). The world, it seems, goes out for a hamburger. McDonald's Canada opened its first restaurant in Moscow just before the collapse of the Soviet Union. That facility had 900 seats and 27 cash registers. The Moscow McDonald's used packaging materials from overseas and cattle and crops raised locally; it opened a 10,000-square-foot distribution center where meat, vegetable, dairy, and bakery products were processed. McDonald's added other restaurants and, by 1990, had invested $50 million in Russia and was serving over 70,000 people a day (Backgrounder 1994; Hume 1990; Sherry 1995). By 2010, 80 percent of the ingredients McDonald's used there was supplied by private businesses in Russia, and the chain had 235 restaurants in the country, employing 25,000 people directly and another 100,000 in its supply chain (Kramer 2010). McDonald's operations in Russia is an example of globalization.

Other examples of the global nature of business include Rainforest Crunch, which is made with Brazil nuts processed in a factory owned and operated in Brazil by indigenous peoples of the Brazilian rain forest. Forty percent of the product gross is returned to finance the enterprise in Brazil. In North America the product is marketed by Cultural Survival, a nonprofit organization based in Cambridge, Massachusetts. Shaman Pharmaceuticals, a joint venture between North American environmental activists and South American indigenous peoples, researches and produces healing and medicinal products, such as antifungal drugs and compounds for diabetes therapy, which are based on indigenous knowledge and made from South American plants (Sherry 1995).

Brand-name products from Europe, Japan, and North America are found all over the world. There is also an active, worldwide business in counterfeit items, known as knockoffs. In 1973, the South Korean government seized $12.5 million in counterfeit goods, including imitation Gucci watches and Chanel bags. The government's greatest difficulty came in trying to dispose of the goods. To store them was costly, to burn or bury them was environmentally problematic, and to give them away with their brand identifications could lead to resale on the streets. The government finally asked for volunteers to assist in removing the brand logos and redistributing the goods (Sherry 1995).

Products are not the only items on the move around the world; culture gets borrowed as well. Santiago Villaveces-Izquierdo described his experience at the headquarters of Foto Japón, a chain of film-developing stores in Colombia that is Colombian-owned and staffed but has borrowed Japanese culture.

> In a shanty part of Bogotá where dust, pollution, and dirt sprout, and among the remains of what used to be a flourishing meat-market spot stands the five-floor building of the central offices of Foto Japón. The building, surrounded by warehouses, small neighborhood liquor stores, and a black market of raw meat and viscera, has the phantasmagoric quality of a ruin among ruins. Inside is a modest and desolate lobby, caught in between two security doors and filled only with a pair of cheap benches, a wooden desk, and a couple of employees dressed in kimonos who welcome and announce the visitors. After passing the second door, a wide staircase leads upstairs through a walking gallery of beautiful Japanese prints and posters from the world's most important museums. On each floor and cutting abruptly the artistic charm, carpets and posted signs remind the visitors to clean their shoes. Arriving at the top floor, one encounters a long white corridor with doors on each side that access either the executives' offices or the company's dining room. It doesn't take long to notice that everyone in the building wears, on top of their everyday garments, a kimono tied with a colored belt, or obi. One soon learns that the color of the obi represents time in the organization and not hierarchy.
>
> The working spaces of Foto Japón are all similar. . . . The windows are all covered with a white cloth framed with thin bamboo sticks; the walls, all white, occasionally have a cluster of framed prints of ancient Japanese art; most of the offices have sliding bamboo doors. . . . Foto Japón's [executive] dining room was not any dif-

ferent from the rest. In between empty white walls, lay a rectangular wooden table with twelve dining places, each with a complete set of bowls of different sizes and painted with Japanese motifs, wooden sticks, sushi, and plenty of tea. Before sitting down I was guided through their daily routine; first we did two minutes of head and neck rotations and limb stretching, then we all sat down and did a three-minute relaxation exercise in which everyone was to clear their mind and rest; finally, I was told, it was prohibited to talk during lunch about anything dealing either with work or unpleasant matters . . . . Lunch was served by three Foto Japón employees who had been trained by the main waiter of Hatsuhana, Bogotá's most famous Japanese restaurant. After cleaning ourselves with hot towels we were offered, as expected, a complete Japanese meal. (Villaveces-Izquierdo 1998:114–115)

Villaveces-Izquierdo went on to interview Juan, one of the owners, Ignacio, a management expert, Margarita, the executive vice president, and Paola, an employee in the human resources division. They further explained the rituals and philosophy the company borrowed from Japan. In this case, a Colombian owned and operated company has adopted Japanese cultural style, including the wearing of kimonos by all employees, even in the retail outlets.

I could use many more examples from around the world to demonstrate this global mixing. As I mentioned in the introduction, examples of globalization are found in every chapter of the book, but it is so important to understand globalization in order to understand twenty-first-century business that I devote this entire chapter to it as well. The global possibility brought by modern technology allows for complex levels of culture borrowing. In this chapter we first look at various kinds of borrowing as products, people, and capital move around the world. Then we examine the ways complex organizations such as national governments, multinational corporations, nonprofits, and transnational organizations (think United Nations, World Trade Organization) partner globally to move their missions forward and, in the process, cause the global movement of products, people, and capital.

CULTURAL ISSUES IN THE MANAGEMENT OF PRODUCTS

Theodore Bestor has described the Tsukiji fish market, a global marketplace in Tokyo (Bestor 1999). Known as *Tokyo no daidokoro*, "Tokyo's pantry," at the time of Bestor's study the market sold $6 billion in fish annually. It was one of 56 officially designated wholesale markets specializing in fish, and it accounted for over 14 percent of the total annual tonnage of fish in this Japanese wholesale system. The market continues to be part of an intricate international fishing industry and reflects the internationalization of cuisine in Japan, a country that is a wealthy, global player in business. The Tsukiji market had its beginnings in the early 1600s when the Tokugawa Shogunate granted privileges to certain fishers who supplied the court with fish in Edo (known as Tokyo since 1868). Most of the modern wholesalers at the market are small-scale traders whose businesses have been in the family for four, seven, even fifteen generations and who are in many cases the direct heirs of those ancient fishers. At the time of Bestor's work, the market contained some 1,677 stalls where fish were bought by retail fishmongers, supermarket buyers, sushi chefs, box lunch makers, hotel caterers, and a few ordinary customers. The market annually sold 450 categories of seafood; this figure, along with subcategories recognized as distinct products, represents some two thousand varieties of fish.

Fish sold in the Tsukiji market comes from all over the world: salmon from Canada and Chile, shrimp from Thailand, blue fin tuna from New York and Istanbul, octopuses from West Africa, and sea urchin roe from Maine (but repackaged in Hokkaido) are but a few of the products that have non-Japanese origins. Market seafood can come from great distances around the world because of modern technology: refrigeration; jet airplanes; and communication systems, such as cellular and smart phones, and the Internet. This has allowed North American fishers to sell tuna to North American and Japanese buyers, who follow the tuna fishers along the Atlantic coast and over into the Mediterranean. They then ship the tuna they buy by jet to the Tokyo market, where it is auctioned along with tuna from the Canary Islands, Sardinia, Turkey, and Australia. In addition to the global shipping of fish, some gourmet dishes in modern Japan would not be possible without modern technology. For example, many varieties of sushi were not possible before refrigeration in the mid-1900s. Not only do the people of Tokyo act as global consumers in eating fish, one of the most traditional of Japanese foods, but the Tsukiji market helps shape the global seafood business as it is one of the largest seafood markets in the world.

Seafood is an important cultural food commodity in Japan, possibly second in importance only to rice. The cultural tastes of the Japanese who eat the fish involve traditional Japanese regional culture, modern national food culture resulting in part from the industrialization of food, and modern Japanese gourmet food culture resulting in part from Japanese wealth. Some of the traditional views of seafood are culturally constructed. For instance, in Osaka, eels are slit along the belly, but in Tokyo, they are slit along the back, because Tokyo was a samurai town and slitting the belly brought to mind ritual suicide. At the Japanese market, sea urchin roe from Hokkaido (one of Japan's northern islands) is preferred over the same delicacy from the US state of Maine, even though the taste of the two is the same. The Hokkaido roe is preferred because the Japanese purchasers perceive it to taste better. This is an example of a culturally constructed value.

Modern Tokyo seafood cuisine is impacted by exposure to foreign cuisines, expansion of scientific nutritional knowledge, and the development of technologies of production, transportation, and processing. Some foreign foods, such as curried rice, have been so adapted by the Japanese that they are no longer considered "foreign," while others are popular adaptations but are still considered foreign, such as sea urchin pizza and fish sausage. Sea urchin pizza is an example of cultural borrowing where the borrowed product, pizza, is adapted to Japanese culture by using sea urchins as a topping. Just as in North America, many foods have become industrialized. Kikkoman is now a global leader in the production of soy sauce, having turned a local craft product into a nationally standardized, manufactured product. What appears in North American supermarkets as "imitation crab meat" is really "extruded pollock," a new industrial food evolved from traditional Japanese fish pastes.

The short of it is this: the globalization of consumer behavior is wide-ranging and complex. As the fish market example illustrates, many issues are involved in bringing fish to the table in Japan. In all this mixing of cultural items, an understanding of the recontextualization of products to fit the new culture of which they are a part is essential. Consequently, it makes sense that anthropologists who are specialists in understanding the cultures and societies of the world can contribute to understanding the issues involved in global business. Everywhere in the world, as members of one culture interact with members of another culture in business transactions, cultural understanding is essential to the success of these transactions.

CULTURAL ISSUES IN THE MANAGEMENT OF PEOPLE

The Tokyo fish market demonstrates the movement of products around the globe, but it is not only products that move, it is human beings as well. As human beings confront new cultures, they learn that their own culture is not the natural culture for all human beings. As businesses employ people from other cultures, both employees and managers face cultural differences. In a study of an Iowa meatpacking plant, Mark Grey (1999) demonstrated how the globalization of business can create this kind of cultural issue. The meatpacking industry needs low labor costs in order to keep profit up, and a common way for a US or Canadian company to do that is to move its factories to coun-

tries where labor costs are low. However, because of government regu-
lations and the logistics of moving products and people, moving the
plant to another country is not always practical. In Iowa, Grey found
that the managers in a meatpacking plant could bring the labor force
to them by hiring migrants from Mexico and elsewhere.

Anthropologists have long worked in migrant populations and
understand much about the issues and patterns of migrant workers
around the world. This understanding can be applied to the Iowa case.
Grey broadens our knowledge by explaining how, in this plant, workplace conditions and employer attitudes contributed to high turnover
and how immigrants used turnover to their advantage. Turnover has
been historically high in the meatpacking business. It was estimated to
average 60 percent in the entire red-meat industry and indeed was at
80 percent annually in the plant Grey studied. The plant managers
wanted to try to bring down high turnover. In 1997 and 1998, Grey con-
sulted with the plant managers on the turnover problem.

In 1996, the plant, which Grey calls Hog Pride, processed over 3.6
million hogs, producing 932.4 million pounds of pork products for a
total in sales of $787.8 million. Hog Pride was the largest employer in
the community, employing 1,900 production and managerial workers,
with a payroll close to $49 million. Latino migrant workers made up
over 50 percent of the workforce with half of those Latino workers coming from a single village of the Michoacán state in Mexico. Lao and
Vietnamese refugees from Asia and Nuer refugees from the Sudan also
were part of the workforce. To appreciate fully the nature of an 80 percent turnover, Grey tells us that on a typical day, one-fourth of the
workforce had been on the job for less than one month and 60 percent
for less than one year. Management had already tackled the high turnover rate by raising wages. This did help; it brought the annual turnover rate down from 120 percent to the 80 percent mentioned earlier.
Wages alone did not seem to be the answer.

Many factors contributed to the high turnover. Meatpacking is the
most dangerous industry in the United States, averaging 44.4 work-
related injuries or illnesses per 100 full-time workers, and injuries contribute to the high turnover. The large numbers of Latino migrants
working in the plant from one state in Mexico provided Grey with an
additional clue to understanding high turnover. The clue lay in the pattern of migration the workers developed. For the migrants, meatpacking jobs were relatively well paying and easy to get. Locals in Iowa, on
the contrary, considered the wages to be insufficient, given the difficulty and danger of the work. For the migrants, once a few migrants
from one village found jobs in a plant, others in the village learned of it
and followed them. This way the migrants could take advantage of the
available jobs and the support network of their relatives and friends as
well. The plant did nothing to recruit immigrants directly, but this

word of mouth recruitment system assured a steady stream of workers. Migrant workers maintained their strong ties with their home communities, and many quit at Christmas and in the spring, in order to go home to attend seasonal festivities.

Plant managers braced themselves for this seasonal turnover. US managers viewed this behavior as irrational. Grey found that migration to the United States for jobs and the subsequent quitting of these jobs were quite rational strategies that migrants used to acquire wealth and then use it to its greatest potential at home in Mexico. The quitting allowed them to return home to reestablish contacts with family and friends. Grey explained to the managers how this strategy actually benefited the plant because it was from the returning workers that prospective migrants learned about the available jobs at the Iowa plant. The fact that the plant did not advertise to get employees was at least partially due to the worker strategy of quitting. After all, over a fourth of the workforce came from the same Mexican town.

While businesspeople/store owners in town fretted over the fact that the migrants did not settle down in their community and purchase their goods and services, the migrants had no incentive to do so. Financially and emotionally the greater incentive was to return to Mexico. With such high turnover, job training was minimal and wages were low; to accommodate these factors, jobs had been deskilled. Grey points out that employees had no ownership of their work because of this deskilling of jobs.

There was a general understanding at the plant that good supervisors, those with good people skills, supervised lines that were more productive and had less turnover. Consequently, the plant offered Dale Carnegie classes to supervisors in an attempt to improve their people skills. About half the supervisors attended. Supervisors were in a no-win situation because they were pressured by their superiors (who had no exposure to the culture of the labor force) to meet production goals but did not have the necessary resources to motivate workers to care more about their jobs. Ninety-one percent of these floor supervisors were Anglo and spoke only English; they had difficulty communicating with the migrant workers (even though the plant employed translators to help with this problem).

Grey explained that many issues were involved in the high turnover, and it would take more than good people skills to reduce turnover. In addition to training in people skills, Grey recommended that supervisors receive mandatory training in cross-cultural skills and that employees receive wage raises, longer training to learn knife skills, and practice butchering before they are placed on the line to "pull their count" (make the required number of cuts per hour). Grey's recommendations would reduce turnover significantly, which would result in higher productivity. Managers responded that these recommended changes were impossible (increasing wages) or unnecessary (the jobs were so deskilled that there was no need for better training). While management wanted to reduce turnover from 80 percent to 60 percent at Hog Pride, they did not perceive a need to reduce it significantly more than that.

The very characteristics of the job that attracted the Latino workers to the work, namely that they could perform it without learning English and could easily get and quit jobs, were also characteristics that allowed the plant to pay low wages. Both the US company's managers and the Mexican migrants employed strategies to maximize their own success, which in turn kept turnover high (Grey 1999). Grey's study demonstrates ways in which cultural factors play a role in businesses that use a global workforce.

CULTURAL ISSUES IN THE MANAGEMENT OF CAPITAL

While many in business assume that it makes no difference whose capital or whose labor is invested in any particular region or product in our global economy, anthropologists would argue otherwise. Labor and capital are components of culture. In the movement of capital, culture can be the clue to who is investing and where they are investing; it often provides the glue that makes investments in some global business work.

Johanna Lessinger (1992), who suggests we need to broaden our understanding of the role of contemporary migration in industrial development, provides an example in which immigrants played an important role in the movement of capital and the globalization of the economy in their former homeland. Beginning in the 1960s, India experienced a large out-migration by its educated, urban elites. In the 1980s, the government of India attempted to benefit from these wealthy expatriates by emphasizing nationalist pride and cultural ties to encourage them to invest in India. Those expatriates understood the advantage of investing in India because they knew it had a low-wage yet skilled labor force and a large consumer market. The Indians living overseas benefited from their cultural knowledge and ties. These investors knew the people and the strategies necessary to negotiate Indian bureaucracy, and they frequently invested in their native regions and hired relatives and friends to oversee their investments. In turn, these overseas investors, when visiting India, helped spread cultural tastes from their new homelands and thus contributed to a global mixing of culture in both their old and new places of residence. Lessinger provides several examples:

Mr. B., based in New York, imports Indian foodstuffs. He sells these retail and acts as a distributor to other Indian grocery shops all over the United States. He uses family ties in Africa (a source of lentils) and in Indian rice-growing areas. Some years ago Mr. B. decided that there was a good market in the United States for a regional variety of home-style hot pickle.

Mr. B. provided the capital that allowed a former pickle supplier to expand his tiny factory outside Bombay. In return for the capital and a share of the profits, Mr. B. is allotted all the factory's output. The factory involves little fancy technology. . . . Mr. B.'s cousin handles the shipping of the pickles and keeps a general eye on the concern. (Lessinger 1992:77)

In another example, a group of South Indian doctors in the United States opened a Western-style hospital and medical research facility in Andhra Pradesh state. They offered building plots to "donor/investors" who would then be able to practice medicine in the modern hospital facility. This served not only as an investment for them but also as a facility that their relatives and they themselves could use for health care should they return to India. Also, it provided medical training for their children and relatives at a cost substantially less than the cost in the United States.

Thus, globalization involves a complex set of relationships that have implications for culture change and business interaction around the world. North America, for example, exports and imports both labor and capital around the world. In all of these interactions, culture plays a role. Lessinger (1992) suggests that neither capital nor labor in the global economy are anonymous and interchangeable. Culture plays a part in whose capital is invested and which labor pool is utilized. Understanding the role of culture increases our understanding of the processes at work in the globalization of business. As we have seen, individuals who migrate out of their countries of origin frequently impact the flow of both labor and capital in their new locations and in their native ones. The Indian examples demonstrate that investors can be defined by culture and the location of investments can be culturally determined.

ORGANIZATIONS AS GLOBAL PARTNERS

Tomoko Hamada's study tracing events in a US–Japanese joint venture in the 1970s and 1980s demonstrates the cultural negotiation of products, labor, and capital in a richly complex global setting (Hamada 1991). Understanding the successes and failures of this joint venture demonstrate the multiple arenas in which cultural factors lurk. While it is impossible in a short space to describe all the junctures

Hamada found where culture was important and where cultural understandings or misunderstandings contributed to the success or failure of
this joint venture, I will describe several of these junctures in order to
demonstrate their importance and complexity.

Until the 1970s, American firms could enter Japan only through
a joint venture with a Japanese firm, and even after the 1970s they frequently sought joint venture arrangements because the Japanese market was so difficult for an outside company to penetrate. The US
company, United American, and the Japanese company, Nippon Kaisha, entered into a joint venture because United American wanted to
gain entrance to the Japanese market. Nippon Kaisha on the other
hand wanted to gain the technology (of plastic wrapping materials) possessed by the North Americans. While the Japanese were not really
interested in a joint venture, the North Americans were unwilling to
sell the technology and insisted instead on the joint venture in order to
gain entrance to the market. The company created by the Nippon Kaisha and United American joint venture (Nippon United) was based in
Japan, with each parent company contributing 50 percent of the capital
and managing it jointly.

Before describing the macro cultural differences, we will touch on
Hamada's description of the many everyday cultural misunderstandings experienced by Japanese and North Americans when they work
together. These are those small behaviors and assumptions to which we
all adhere, thinking they are common for all humans, when actually
they are behaviors and assumptions specific to our own culture. For
instance, an American manager asked for decaffeinated coffee at a
lunch hosted by his Japanese counterparts. This caused great embar-
rassment among the Japanese hosts, who did not have decaffeinated
coffee available. In Japan, all needs of the guests at such a lunch should
be met by the hosts, and their failure to anticipate this desire for decaffeinated coffee indicated a poor job of preparing for their guests. The
American's seemingly innocent request was singling out the Japanese
hosts' failure to be prepared. Thus, while to the Americans this was a
minor incident, to the Japanese it was a major issue indicating the
hosts had failed in their duties.

Another example was the importance of corner offices with many
windows. In the United States, such an office typically indicates that
the occupant is a high-level manager. In Japan, however, it indicates
that the occupant is being moved out of the promotion ladder. Managers of importance are placed in the thick of the action, not closeted off
in the corner away from the work and decision making. A Japanese
manager could easily misunderstand the symbolic significance of that
corner office to an American. As a third example, the way in which a
Japanese businessperson says "no" can easily be taken for "yes" or
"maybe" by a North American. To say "no," he may say "yes" to the

planned undertaking but follow the yes with a lengthy explanation of the problems, or he may say "I will consider it." Both of these responses mean "no" but allow both parties to save face. They can be misunderstood by Americans.

However, at Nippon United there were many cultural misunderstandings much more complex than these daily assumptions and behaviors. An important difference in Japanese and US organizational structure made it generally difficult for outsiders to penetrate the Japanese market, and it also accounted for many of the cultural misunderstandings at Nippon United. Japanese organizational structure is a cultural system that is very different from that in the United States and Canada. In Japan, companies are organized into a few large groups; each group is composed of a large company, such as Mitsubishi, and its "offspring." The company, Dai-Nippon, which Hamada studied, had over 100 "child" companies under it. One of these was Nippon Kaisha. Dai-Nippon owned 69 percent of Nippon Kaisha, and Nippon Kaisha in turn was a parent company to some 33 smaller companies, one of which was the joint venture company of Nippon United. Nippon Kaisha owned 50 percent of that company. In addition to this structure, there were independent subcontractors involved with Dai-Nippon, which means that the Dai-Nippon group was made up of some 6,000 companies of various sizes. So, from a Japanese perspective, the joint venture company was one of some 6,000 companies related to each other in a hierarchical structure.

Approximately 40 percent of Japan's total industrial capital was controlled by groups such as Dai-Nippon. This explains one reason foreign companies had such a difficult time penetrating the Japanese market. The Japanese preferred doing business with other companies in their family group; one-third of Nippon Kaisha's business, for instance, was with partner firms. As part of this structure, workers and capital were moved among firms closely tied in the group. Thus, not only company structure but also personnel were controlled by this organizational principle. In addition, Japanese employment policies emphasized lifetime employment. The firing of employees was unlikely.

As you probably already suspect, the Japanese and American organizational structures were at odds. North American businesses are not structured according to the "family" hierarchy found in Japan. The different organizational structures dictated different management styles. For the most part, the Japanese managers of the new joint venture company, Nippon United, were individuals from Nippon Kaisha, its Japanese parent company, and their views on growth of the joint venture were subsidiary to their interest in the growth of the larger Japanese group of companies of which Nippon United was a part. On the other hand, the US managers were interested in profits for the joint venture company *only*, as the US parent company expected the joint venture to sink or swim on its own merits. For the US side, the joint venture needed to turn a profit as quickly as possible. This was important not only to the survival of the company but also to the career advancement of the US managers. No Japanese managers' careers were in danger if the joint venture profits were low. For them the most important factor was maintaining good relations with the parent companies and promoting solidarity in the Dai-Nippon group. They were willing to forego quick profits in order to work on market expansion. Thus, managers in the joint venture company had different goals depending on the organizational structure common in their home cultures.

Another of the areas of cultural clash that developed concerned the transfer of the technology for making the plastic wrap. I described this briefly in chapter 4. In setting up a new factory to produce the plastic wrap materials, the US engineers trained the Japanese engineers in transfer of the technology. Lack of communication about important details is a common problem in situations of transferring technology. For example, in the United States the layout of the machines on the factory floor was designed for maximum time saving during the production process. In Japan, where land is expensive and space is at a premium, the Japanese engineers redesigned the layout of the machines so that they would take up less space. The US engineers had not communicated the reason behind the floor layout, assuming that the Japanese would have no reason to alter it. The result was that the close proximity of the machines inhibited maintenance, work space, and movement of equipment, causing the factory to be less efficient than its North American counterpart. In addition, the US engineers neglected to tell the Japanese that they checked and cleaned the machines when contamination caused the plastic wrap to have an imperfect appearance due to trapped dust particles and that the plant buildings in the United States were sealed against dust. The plant building in Japan had not been built to prevent all dust from entering, and expensive repairs to the building had to be made. The quality of the wrap improved after the Japanese learned about the importance of frequent machine cleaning.

The US managers determined that the production problems were due as much to poor management as to miscommunications in technology transfer. They told the Japanese they wished to fire the plant manager and replace him with someone who was more dynamic, younger, and more aggressive. Changing the plant manager went against the values of Japanese management, but eventually they agreed, and a younger Japanese manager was given the job. Later, the US managers wanted to promote this young manager to the job of a full-time president of Nippon United. What the US managers did not understand was that to give a junior manager such a high-status job would be ineffectual in the Japanese hierarchy. The young manager would have to deal as an equal with other managers senior to him. He did not have the working relationships with them that a manager at their same level had. No matter how capable, he would not be able to get the others to work with him and thus would be ineffectual. The US approach, which exemplified the US values of individual responsibility and short-term profits, clashed with the Japanese approach, exemplified by valuing lifelong employment, climbing the corporate ladder in step with one's colleagues, and considering the performance of any single company with regard to the way it fit into its larger family of companies. The Japanese did not consider quick profits to be important.

In Japan, sales of the new plastic wrap were low. The US managers considered this to be partly a result of poor product quality, which resulted from the problems with the production process. The Japanese insisted that even when the product was produced at US standards, sales in Japan would still be low. In Japan the appearance of a product is expected to be perfect, whereas in the United States, small, visible imperfections in the plastic wrap, which did not inhibit its function, were acceptable to buyers. The US managers decided the problem in Japan was that the Japanese just did not know how to market the product. Actually, what was at issue was a fundamental difference in culture. The US and Japanese managers, together, would never be able to market the product well enough to convince the Japanese to change their cultural ways. It actually made more sense to refine the product so its appearance would be acceptable in the Japanese market.

All of these misunderstandings and disagreements related to the difference in how the Japanese and the US managers culturally constructed their understanding of organizational structure, management style and goals, general values, and behaviors. An anthropologist's role in assisting companies undertaking a multinational joint venture is to help them identify and negotiate the cultural differences so that those differences do not become barriers to success.

THE IMPORTANCE OF ORGANIZATIONS IN THE PROCESS OF GLOBALIZATION

The US–Japanese joint venture exemplifies how business organizations join together across national borders to achieve their goals. Today, many complex organizations, be they corporations, nonprofits, or government agencies, are forming transnational partnerships. This is an important process of globalization. Consequently, I wish to provide one last example of the cultural negotiation of products, labor, and capital among organizations in order to underscore the importance of globalization and the value of organizational anthropology in understanding it.

In 2002, I conducted a study of a hospital in the Kingdom of Saudi Arabia (Kingdom) (Jordan 2011). As an organizational anthropologist, I was fascinated by the fact that this hospital employed people holding passports from over 60 countries, and I was interested in how that worked in an organizational context. What was it like to have people from Saudi Arabia, Somalia, South Africa, India, Norway, and the United States all working side by side? Did the presence of over 60 different cultures cause confusion? What I found was not only a story of cultures interacting but also an example of the processes of globalization at work. To tell this story, I need to present some background on the Kingdom and the hospital itself.

The hospital began operating in 1975. This was a time when the Kingdom had few modern health facilities. In fact there were only 74 hospitals in the entire country, and it is a country one-third the size of the continental United States. Imagine, only 74 hospitals in an area larger than the US region east of the Mississippi River. How could this be so in 1970? Let me explain.

Saudi Arabia is a relatively young state. In the 1930s, when the Kingdom was formed, it was a poor country with few resources other than camels and dates. It was a traditional Arab country—education centered on learning the Qur'an, and transportation was by camel. The rapid rate of change the Kingdom has undergone in the last 70 years, even the last 30 years, is difficult to appreciate. Today, the Kingdom is a modern country with shopping malls, traffic jams, marble and steel buildings, and Starbucks and Saks Fifth Avenue stores. Perhaps it is easier to understand this transformation though human stories. Living in the Kingdom today are people who have lived through the transition. Consider Sara, a not-so-old grandmother, who crossed the country on camelback in her youth and as an adult crossed the Atlantic on the Concorde airplane. Or, there is the case of Abdul Rahman, a computer specialist in his mid-40s who speaks several languages fluently and was schooled in the US. He lived in a traditional adobe village as a child and slept on the roof in the summer to catch the cool air. This was a village with narrow dirt streets designed only for foot traffic and animal-drawn carts. The village is now a historic landmark sitting beside the modern, concrete, steel, and marble city of Riyadh.

Using its oil wealth, the government of Saudi Arabia was determined to modernize the country, and it began doing so in earnest in the 1970s. Consequently, the hospital I studied was opened with 120 beds on the edge of the desert, on the outskirts of Riyadh, the capital city, in 1975. One of the employees remembers:

> People used to come and sit out in front of the hospital under the street lights because there weren't any lights out this far and they would sit there and read their books at night. There was no airport out here. We couldn't get a taxi here. . . . Too far out of town. There

was very little food in the grocery stores. This was in 1975. There was not much food here. You couldn't make a telephone call easily. You couldn't buy a flower. Now they import flowers from Amsterdam and you can get anything you want over night.

The Kingdom had few trained physicians, no medical schools or other trained medical personnel in 1975. Consequently, the Saudi government partnered with a US firm, Hospital Corporation of America (HCA), to set up and run this hospital. Thus, a US corporation created the working hospital—put in place all the procedures, hired the staff, and managed the development of a modern health care facility. Doctors and nurses were hired primarily from Europe and North America. Employees remember: "Almost 100 percent of the staff was American at that time. . . . The Americans were here and they put in an American system, turnkey." Meanwhile, the Kingdom sent its most promising students to Europe and the US to attend college and medical school. The students' tuitions and living expenses were paid by the government with the understanding that the students would return to practice medicine in the Kingdom.

The hospital also partnered with other Western medical organizations. For example, in 1978 it partnered with Baylor College of Medicine, Houston, Texas, to begin performing cardiac surgery. The partnership with Baylor would continue until 1985 when cardiology services became offered entirely by the Kingdom's in-house medical staff. The management of HCA ended in 1981, and Saudis took the lead in hospital administration. The hospital has continued to develop international partnerships, however. In fact any modern, cutting-edge hospital does this.

An example of one of these partnerships is its relationship with CBAY, a US company. In 2003 the hospital contracted with CBAY for medical transcription. The Kingdom had few trained medical transcriptionists and tried to recruit them from the United States, South Africa, and Asia but with little luck. Faced with a backlog of transcription needs, the hospital contracted with CBAY to handle medical transcription. Each day they transmitted their medical records electronically to CBAY in the United States, where records were in turn transmitted to India, where transcriptionists actually transcribed them. Then the records were transmitted back to the United States, checked for errors, and sent on to Saudi Arabia to the hospital, *all* within 24 hours. The administrator for clinical services learned of CBAY at the Health Care Information and Management Systems Society annual meeting in the United States, another transnational connection.

In 2003 the last non-Saudi administrator, a US citizen, left the hospital, and by then over 50 percent of the physicians were Saudi. The hospital was staffed by 7,488 employees of 63 different nationalities, and they proudly refer to themselves as a "mini United Nations." Saudis made up the largest percentage of the workforce at 38 percent, followed by workers from the Philippines (17 percent), the Sudan (8 percent), Canada (6 percent), India (4 percent), and the United States and South Africa (3 percent each). Many saw this cultural mix as a good environment.

Others describe the kinds of cultural clashes this involves. For example, the following perceptions are culled from interviews with nurses: (1) British doctors clash with American nurses because the United Kingdom has a more rigid system than the United States. British doctors do not expect nurses to question them. (2) English nurses are not taught to do a physical assessment (listen to breathing and heart, check pulse, and so on) when a patient first arrives at the hospital, while US nurses are. (3) Indian nurses do not have the clinical experience or nursing education for this kind of high-tech hospital. (4) Filipinos are excellent at cardiac and pediatric specialties.

In addition to the cultural issues at the hospital, I found the partnerships with organizations around the world to be significant in understanding how the processes of globalization work. Transnational partnerships, such as the ones the hospital had with HCA, Baylor College of Medicine, and CBAY remain essential for conducting business efficiently. Actually, no world-class medical organization today is without continual, transnational partnerships, as cutting-edge medicine is a global business. Outsourcing in health care as well as in a host of other businesses has become a way of life in Saudi Arabia and a way of life around the world. The hospital is a story of movement—of people, as workers from over 60 nations streamed into the hospital for jobs; of products, such as medical equipment; and of capital, as the Saudi government contracted with other organizations. It is also a story of the complex links among governments, educational institutions, transnational corporations, and other forms of organizations that are created in order to fulfill the missions of the various organizations and in doing so fuel the global movement of people, products, and capital.

CONCLUSION

In this chapter we have looked at globalization from an anthropological perspective. Global product movement is an intricate and complex process of borrowing and change. In the Tokyo fish market example, we saw how fish (products) are moved around the globe. The acceptance of these products in cultures other than the ones of their origin depends on how well the products fit into the receiving culture. The receiving culture may alter the way the products are perceived and used to make them fit. The availability of new products can in turn bring about culture change.

In the Iowa meatpacking example, we saw how people move globally. Here, understanding the culture of the labor force as well as that of the company can provide solutions to labor problems and in turn increase productivity. In the case of expatriate Indians who were investing in their country of origin, it was money that was moving globally, and again, culture was the key to who was investing where. The example of the Japan–US joint venture demonstrates the cultural issues involved in the movement of products (plant equipment), people (management and staff), and capital (funds from two parent companies). Here the issues are complex and intertwined as management styles and national culture are tied to all aspects of success. Understanding how to negotiate a global business environment is vital for success in today's economy, and anthropology provides tools for that understanding. Finally, the hospital in Saudi Arabia is an example of how transnational organizations combine, split, and sometimes recombine in new ways as they partner to achieve mutual goals across the globe. In doing so, they initiate and perpetuate the flow of people, products, and capital.

Anthropologists are well trained to study the types of global interactions exemplified in this chapter and to tackle the cultural problems these interactions provoke. Intensified globalization is one of the defining characteristics of the twenty-first century, and anthropology should be at the forefront in analyzing and solving the critical problems this involves.

Chapter Ten

The Importance
of Holism

Museum attendance, decoupled systems,
and a cup of coffee . . .

Many business anthropologists never mention that important
anthropological construct, culture, in their work. They use the perspectives of anthropology, however, to understand an array of issues in
organizational work and in consumer behavior. A key feature of the
anthropological perspective that is important to business anthropologists is *holism*—pulling back from the specific problem, event, or situation under study and putting it in a larger context. Anthropologists
are trained to look at questions larger than the one they are being
asked to answer.

For example, when Susan Squires (2002) conducted the evaluation of video conferencing equipment described in chapter 7, she used
a holistic perspective. The organization assumed it wanted video conferencing. It seemed like a "no-brainer" that if managers on different
sides of the globe could get together via video conferencing, the need for
expensive travel would be reduced. However, when Squires was asked
to help the managers determine which brand of equipment best suited
their needs, she pulled back from the specific question she was being
asked to answer and looked at larger issues.

For starters, she placed the question of what brand of equipment
in a larger context: What do the managers need this for, and will they
use it? Then she organized the evaluation of equipment, which was
described in chapter 7. As you recall, she learned that managers stated

they loved the equipment, but in actuality they did not use it. During a conference call, they quickly turned off the video camera. On the basis of Squires's study, the company decided not to purchase video conferencing equipment at all. Had Squires just answered the question she was asked (Which brand should the company purchase?), the company would have bought equipment, and the managers would not have used it. Squires did not begin with the assumption that the company needed the equipment. She started by learning if they needed it. In looking at the bigger picture, she was looking at the issue holistically.

A nonprofit community hospital on the East Coast was receiving too many complaints from both patients and emergency room (ER) staff about the long time it took to get a bed for an ER patient who needed to be admitted. Irwin Press (1997) was called in as a consultant to see if he could fix the problem. By interviewing and conducting focus groups with numerous individuals including the trustees, the CEO, senior management, inpatient managers, floor nurses, ER doctors, and housekeeping staff, he learned of multiple problems. Everyone thought the problem was someone else's fault. ER nurses thought housekeeping was not getting the rooms ready fast enough. Housekeeping felt they were preparing rooms quickly and that the problem was that the floor nurses responsible for notifying ER when rooms were ready were not doing so promptly. Both floor nurses and housekeeping blamed the attending physicians for allowing patients to stay until late in the day when relatives got off work to pick them up; this meant rooms were not available during the day. ER doctors blamed housekeeping, and so on and so on.

The turf issues involved in getting beds for ER patients promptly cut across at least five different staff entities. Press learned this because he interviewed at all levels of the organization. With an anthropologist's sense of the holistic nature of problems, he knew to pull back and put the problem he was asked to address in a larger context. He did not interview *only* patients and ER staff, who were the two groups who had complained about the problem. He knew the problem would involve other groups as well. Ultimately he prepared a report for the hospital that helped management see the integrated nature of this problem. It involved issues of organizational structure, empowerment, and role definition among five different groupings (Press 1997).

Another example of holism can be found in Carole Duhaime, Annamma Joy, and Christopher Ross's (1995) study at Montreal's Museum of Contemporary Art. Their charge was to provide suggestions that would increase attendance. Using participant observation and interviews, they came up with the following conclusions:

1. The objects on view in the museum possessed not only a meaning placed on them by the artists who created them but also a meaning placed on them by the museum. In displaying the

objects, the museum authenticated them as art. In the way in which the museum displayed the objects, it interpreted them. The museum then created a meaning for the objects in the eyes of the viewer. For example, exhibits in prime museum space with radio transmitters for self-guided tours were being accorded a place of greater status than exhibits in less prominent places and with no tours. The higher-status exhibits had higher attendance.

2. Visitors came to the museum with different interests and needs. The museum-goer's previous experience in museums, especially in childhood, played a role in his comfort, interest, and participation in adult museum-going experiences. Some of the types of viewers the anthropologists found were (a) artists, (b) tourists, (c) children, and (d) senior citizens. In each group, expectations for the museum experience were different, and the museum could serve the patrons better by working toward providing each group with different experiences. All visitors did not have the same level of sophistication regarding the work they were viewing. For example, for the artists who wished to closely examine materials, substances, color, and form, the museum could provide more in-depth information about these characteristics of the works. Considering these different audiences when preparing exhibits could increase attendance.

3. Furthermore, observation of the way the museum space was used uncovered several areas that could be improved. Upon entry, visitors were frequently confused about where to go; there were few signs to direct them and no visible attendant to ask. The café was a popular spot among visitors, but its location was hard to find, and on weekends it did not have enough cups and saucers to satisfy the requests of its clientele. Improving signage and better equipping the café could improve the visitors' experience and improve attendance.

Thus, the museum experience must be viewed holistically. The café, museum store, brochures, attitude of attendants and guards, as well as the exhibits themselves, played a role in the museum-goer's experience. By conducting a study on use of museum space, a study of the meaning of museum objects, and a study of the types of visitors, Duhaime, Joy, and Ross (1995) used a holistic approach to solving the problem of how to increase museum attendance. They knew the answer could not be found by just surveying or interviewing visitors about the museum experience.

Holism was important in a study by Elizabeth Briody and Marietta Baba (1991) of overseas assignments at General Motors (GM). When GM employees who were sent overseas came back to North

America, some of them reintegrated easily into the GM world and others did not. Some individuals had trouble with "reverse culture shock." Having adjusted to an overseas culture, they had trouble readjusting to their home culture. Some had trouble reintegrating into the work environment in North America either because of the unavailability of an appropriate job or because of possessing outdated skills. Some suffered a loss of status and promotions due to the overseas absence. Others, however, had a smooth, easy reintegration into the North American workforce at GM. Briody and Baba were asked to figure out why the repatriation experience was difficult for some and easy for others. They took a holistic anthropological approach to the problem.

Looking beyond the individual returning employees, they learned that an important factor in successful repatriation was GM's organizational structure. Within GM there were two types of organizational structures, which Briody and Baba termed the *coupled system* and the *decoupled system*. In coupled systems, a single structural unit at GM contained both domestic and international subunits. In decoupled systems, the whole unit was either domestic or international. In a coupled system, the overseas employees never leave their organizational unit. They retain their status in the hierarchy of their unit. Because their overseas job is within their unit, managers in the North American segment of the unit understand the significance of the job and the skills the individual is developing overseas. Thus, reintegration back into North America was smooth, as the individual had never left his organizational home. By contrast, in decoupled systems, the individual going overseas leaves her North American organizational unit. Upon return, the home unit may not understand or appreciate the skills developed in the overseas assignment and does not credit the individual for that work time, because the job was not in the home unit. One manager explained, "Once you leave the North American Car Group [a decoupled system] to go and work for any overseas car operation, you drop out of the head count of the North American Car Group and you are replaced by someone else."

In this study, Briody and Baba were not studying culture or consumer behavior. They were using anthropological perspectives, however. They looked at the issue of differential ease of repatriation and found that GM organizational structure was a significant factor in understanding the differences. Their holistic perspective, looking at the organization as an integrated system, allowed them to see how a structural issue in the organization as a whole affected individuals moving back to North America from overseas assignments.

When I grab a quick cup of coffee before heading off to a long meeting, I am thinking only of getting that caffeine boost to keep me going through the meeting; I am not thinking of the worldwide implications of my coffee consumption—that is, I'm not thinking about coffee in a holistic way. However, in the past several decades there has been a dramatic change in coffee consumption patterns in North America. Coffee in the United States used to be sold almost solely in cans in the supermarket. The business was dominated by large food industries like Proctor and Gamble and General Foods. By comparison to today's products, the coffees were quite tasteless, and consumer choices were limited to brand and type of grind. This was a time in the United States when food products were sold by large corporate entities, like General Foods, and marketing strategists considered price the most important factor in the successful marketing of coffee. The notion that taste was less important to the consumer than price was widely held in the sales of everything from coffee to apples.

From the 1960s into the 1980s, coffee consumption in the United States declined. Coffee drinkers tended to be older, causing rising concern in the industry over how to attract the coffee drinkers of the future, the 20-somethings. Added to this were the woes caused by the 1975 frost in Brazil, which drove the price of coffee up. What resulted was the growth of a new coffee industry that happened more or less outside the arena of mass marketing. With the cost of coffee up, expensive specialty roasts became only slightly more expensive than the mass-produced products. While the giants in the field controlled most coffee production and distribution to grocery stores, there had always been a specialty market that serviced restaurants and offices. That specialty market was outside of the dominant, standardized, mass production of coffee in vacuum-packed cans.

The specialty market provided a base for the beginnings of a new movement in coffee consumption, which began to take hold in the 1980s and grew into the specialty big business we see today, with Starbucks and other coffee shops and even grocery stores stocking specialty types of coffees alongside those longtime prevalent brands. Now consumers in North America can choose from any number of types of coffees grown all over the world that have different strengths and flavors. Yet, understanding marketing and consumer behavior in this instance is not limited to understanding what people want in a coffee. The new coffee drinkers, including those 20-somethings, see themselves as expressing their individuality and also returning to a purer time when coffee was sold by bulk in barrels or burlap sacks at the general store rather than in metal or plastic containers by brands developed by a global industry and sold through grocery store chains. William Roseberry and his colleagues (1995) have provided a detailed study of this change in the coffee industry in an analysis that highlights the issues of a global political economy.

The new coffee industry was an international business that required not only new types of consumers but also changes in international trade agreements, habits of growers on the other side of the world, and new organizational distribution mechanisms. Specialty roasters had difficulty getting small shipments of green (unroasted) coffee. The old industrial giants had preferred large shipments, as mass production profited from working in large quantities. Trade organizations, like the National Coffee Association and the Specialty Coffee Association of America, played an important role as lobbyists of governments and promoters of the trade. The rules in place as a result of international trade agreements were too rigid to accommodate the growing demands of the specialty coffee business. There was a realization as early as 1981 that the coffee industry needed to develop specialty niches and market different types of coffee products accordingly, when the industry had always been driven by standardization. All of these influences impacted the resurgence in coffee drinking, which the new specialty coffee market enjoys (Roseberry et al. 1995). Roseberry's study exemplifies the anthropologists' use of holism. He places coffee production and consumption in the bigger picture, tracing the global connections that impact my ability to purchase that quick cup of coffee.

CONCLUSION

Remember the story of the blind men and the elephant? Each blind man felt the elephant to determine what sort of creature this was. One felt the tail, another the foot, and a third the trunk. As a result, each imagined the animal differently because each was basing his understanding of the whole elephant from his experience with just a part of the elephant (tail, foot, or trunk). None imagined the elephant correctly because none had experience with the whole elephant. Anthropologists are trained to look for the whole. So in answering a question, we pull back and look for the whole in which the question is embedded. Just as we understand that culture is an integrated system, we understand how issues are frequently integrated with other issues so that to understand museum attendance, for example, one must look at use of space, types of visitors, and placement of objects. Or in order to understand different repatriation experiences among GM employees, one must look at larger issues including GM's overall organizational structure. A holistic perspective is one of anthropology's important contributions to business.

Chapter Eleven

Where Do We Go from Here?

We'll always be in business . . .

In this introduction to the field of business anthropology, we examined the history of the field and the ethical issues that affect all anthropologists (especially those that affect business anthropologists). We considered anthropological work in consumer behavior, marketing, and product design. We also looked at anthropologists' contributions to understanding a wide variety of organizations and at issues involving globalization and diversity. Anthropological techniques, which include those "get-to-know" people techniques, provide ways of seeing organizations that are different from those used in other disciplines. For example, the anthropological focus on culture identifies an organization's cultural constructs and groupings, as well as the ways cultural boundaries are negotiated and renegotiated at multiple levels.

We discussed the importance of holism—the ability to pull back from a specific question and place it in a larger context so we can unpack the complex, interrelated issues of which the question is a part. If the unit of analysis is a branch of a company, we look at the whole company and its market environment to understand the issues in that branch. If the unit of analysis is a product distributed worldwide, we look at the product in the local market to understand how the product is recontextualized in each new political, economic, and social arena in which it is placed. We pay attention to how the product is defined in terms of everything from local family relationships to political power stances, for example.

James Peacock (1997), in an address to the American Anthropological Association, stated:

> Anthropology is everywhere, implicitly and potentially, because of its scope; . . . we address most human issues. This is our primary contribution, this holistic and comparative insight into human diversity and commonality, which together with such practices as participant observation, gives us a distinctive critical perspective. (Peacock 1997:10)

The subject matter of anthropology is found wherever there are people. No wonder business is an apt venue. As the world becomes even smaller with continued globalization, our skills will be more important.

When I look into the future, I see only more work for business anthropologists. I see business anthropology as a growth field in the practice of anthropology, a field that will continually contribute to the understanding of human issues. We should heed the call of Marc Edelman and Angelique Haugerud who plead: "anthropologists would be well placed to explore how markets and the corporations and state and supra-national institutions that influence and administer them actually work" (2005:18). Our world of the future will contain only more multinational organizational presence and more globalized products. Do anthropologists really want to leave the analysis and critique of these phenomena to others? When our discipline provides the skills to understand the complexity and the moral issues involved in such globalization, do we wish to opt out of the dialogue? If as anthropologists we are to make our work relevant and our voices a part of the multinational conversation on the pressing issues in our contemporary world, we must engage in business anthropology.

Whether working for nonprofit or for-profit organizations, we bring every voice to the table by including the low-level employee and the isolated consumer, and we promote intercultural understanding by understanding the value in diverse groups. Because we focus more than most on bringing underrepresented groups into the discussion, we must engage in business anthropology. To be a business anthropologist does not in itself represent a stance for or against business, but it does represent a willingness to engage in the dialogue that illuminates solutions to problems and new ways of seeing old realities; it is fast becoming the defining dialogue of our times. Anthropologists have a responsibility to contribute their knowledge to this worldwide conversation. As we champion consumers, foster human-centered organizations, and promote cultural diversity, we help make the world a better place. I hope the students of today who are the anthropologists of tomorrow will join in delivering our message on the global stage.

Bibliography

Aguilera, Francisco E. 1996. Is Anthropology Good for the Company? *American Anthropologist* 98(4): 735–742.

American Anthropological Association. 1998. Code of Ethics of the American Anthropological Association Approved June 1998. http://www.aaanet.org/committees/ethics/ethicscode.pdf (accessed 2/28/12).

American Anthropological Association. Draft Code of Ethics. http://www.aaanet.org/cmtes/ethics/proposed-revised-code-of-ethics-for-public-review.cfm (accessed 2/28/12).

American Anthropological Association. CEAUSSIC Releases Final Report on Army HTS Program. www.aaanet.org/issues/policy-advocacy/CEAUSSIC-Releases-Final-Report-on-Army-HTS-Program (accessed 2/28/12).

Anderson, Ken, and Rogério de Paula. 2006. We We We All the Way Home: The "We" Effect in Transitional Spaces. *EPIC 2006*, pp. 62–75. American Anthropological Association.

Appadurai, Arjun. 1986. *The Social Life of Things: Commodities in Cultural Perspective.* Cambridge, UK: Cambridge University Press.

Appadurai, Arjun. 1988. How to Make a National Cuisine: Cookbook in Contemporary India. *Comparative Studies in Society and History* 30(1): 3–24.

Applebaum, K. 1992. "I Feel Coke": Why the Japanese Study English. *Asian Thought and Society* 17(49): 18–30.

Applebaum, Herbert. 1984. *Work in Market and Industrial Societies.* Albany: State University of New York Press.

Aracury, Thomas A., and Sara A. Quandt. 1999. Participant Recruitment for Qualitative Research: A Site-Based Approach to Community Research in Complex Societies. *Human Organization* 58(2): 128–133.

Arnould, Eric J. 2001. Introduction to the Special Issue. *Journal of Contemporary Ethnography* 30(4): 359–364.

Arnould, Eric J., and Craig J. Thompson. 2005. Consumer Culture Theory (CCT): Twenty Years of Research. *Journal of Consumer Research* 31(4) (March): 868–882.

Arnould, Eric, Linda Price, and Cele Otnes. 1999. Making Magic Consumption: A Study of White-Water River Rafting. *Journal of Contemporary Ethnography* 28(1): 33–68.

Baba, Marietta L. 1986. Business and Industrial Anthropology: An Overview. *National Association for the Practice of Anthropology.* Volume 2. Washington, DC: American Anthropological Association.

Baba, Marietta L. 1989. Local Knowledge Systems in Advanced Technology Organizations. In *Strategic Management in High Technology Firms,* L. Gomes-Mejia and M. Lawless, (eds.), pp. 57–75. Greenwich, CT: JAI Press.

Baba, Marietta L. 1995. A Biography of Edward T. Hall. *Journal of Applied Behavioral Science* 31(2): 117–18.

Backgrounder. 1994. McDonald's Corporate Communication. February.

Baker, Lee D. 1995. Racism in Professional Settings: Forms of Address as Clues to Power Relationships. *Journal of Applied Behavioral Science* 31(2): 186–201.

Barnett, Steven. 1992. *The Nissan Report.* New York: Doubleday.

Batteau, Allen. 2000. Anthropology with an Altitude. *Anthropology News* 41(5): 19–20.

Batteau, Allen W. 2001. The Anthropology of Aviation and Flight Safety. *Human Organization* 60(3): 201–211.

Batteau, Allen. 2010. *Technology and Culture.* Long Grove, IL: Waveland Press.

Beebe, James. 2000. *Rapid Assessment Process: Intensive, Team-based Qualitative Inquiry.* Walnut Creek, CA: AltaMira Press.

Ben-Ari, Eyal, and Efrat El-Ron. 2002. Blue Helmets and White Armor: Multi-Nationalism and Multi-Culturalism among UN Peacekeeping Forces. *City and Society* 13(2): 271–302.

Bennett, John. 1954. Interdisciplinary Research and the Concept of Culture. *American Anthropologist* 56: 169–179.

Bennett, Linda, T. J. Ferguson, J. Anthony Paredes, et al. 2006. *Final Report: Practicing Advisory Work Group (PAWG).* Arlington, VA: American Anthropological Association.

Bestor, Theodore. 1999. Wholesale Sushi: Culture and Commodity in Tokyo's Tsukiji Market. In *Theorizing the City: The New Urban Anthropology Reader,* Setha M. Lowe (ed.), pp. 201–242. New Brunswick, NJ: Rutgers University Press.

Beyerstein, Lindsay. 2007. Anthropologists on the Front Lines. *Truthout,* 30 November. www.truthout.org/docs_2006/120107G.html (accessed 12/3/2007).

Blomberg, Jeanette, et al. 1993. Ethnographic Field Methods and Their Relation to Design. In *Participatory Design: Principles and Practices,* D. Schuler and A. Namioka (eds.), pp. 123–155. Hillsdale, NJ: Lawrence Erlbaum.

Borgatti, Stephen P., M. G. Everett, and L. C. Freeman. 2002. *Ucinet 6 for Windows: Software for Social Network Analysis.* Cambridge, MA: Analytic Technologies.

Borofsky, Robert. 1993. *Assessing Cultural Anthropology.* New York: McGraw-Hill.

Bourdieu, Pierre. 1977. *Outline of a Theory of Practice.* Cambridge, UK: Cambridge University Press.

Brennen, Mary Yoko, and Mark W. Fruin. 1999. Cultural Alienation in Today's Multinational Work Arenas: Organizational Consequences from Globalization. *Practicing Anthropology* 21(4): 20–27.

Briody, Elizabeth K. 2013. Managing Conflict in Organizational Partnerships. In *A Companion to Organizational Anthropology,* Douglas Caulkins and Ann T. Jordan (eds.). Oxford, UK: Wiley-Blackwell.

Briody, Elizabeth K., and Marietta L. Baba. 1991. Explaining Differences in Repatriation Experiences: The Discovery of Coupled and Decoupled Systems. *American Anthropologist* 93(2): 322–343.

Briody, Elizabeth K., and Judith Beeber Chrisman. 1991. Cultural Adaptation on Overseas Assignments. *Human Organization* 50: 264–282.

Briody, Elizabeth K., Robert Trotter II, and Tracy L. Meerwarth. 2010. *Transforming Culture: Creating and Sustaining a Better Manufacturing Organization.* New York: Palgrave Macmillan.

Britan, Gerald M. 1981. *Bureaucracy and Innovation.* Beverly Hills: Sage.

Britan, Gerald M., and Ronald Cohen. 1980. Toward an Anthropology of Formal Organizations. In *Hierarchy and Society,* G. M. Britan and R. Cohen (eds.), pp. 9–30. Philadelphia: Institute for the Study of Human Issues.

Brown, John Seely, and Paul Duguid. 1991. Organizational Learning and Communities-of-Practice: Toward a Unified View of Working, Learning, and Innovation. *Organization Science* 2(1): 40–57.

Burt, R. S., and M. J. Minor. 1983. *Applied Network Analysis: A Methodological Introduction.* Morristown, NJ: General Learning Press.

136   Bibliography

Caglar, Ayse S. 1995. *McDoner: Doner Kebap* and the Social Positioning Struggle of Ger- man Turks. *In Marketing in a Multicultural World*, J. A. Costa and G. J. Bamossy (eds.), pp. 209–230. Thousand Oaks, CA: Sage.

Cardew Kersey, Jennifer. 2009. *Translating Virtual Ethnography from Academia into Market Research: A Framework*. Master's Practicum. Denton, Texas: University of North Texas.

Carrier, J. G. 1993. The Rituals of Christmas Giving. In *Unwrapping Christmas*, D. Miller (ed.), pp. 55–74. Oxford, UK: Clarendon.

Caulkins, Douglas, and Elaine Weiner. 1998. Finding a Work Culture that Fits: Egalitar- ian Manufacturing Firms in Mid Wales. *Anthropology of Work Review* 19(1): 27–31.

Caulkins, Douglas, and Ann T. Jordan, eds. 2013. *A Companion to Organizational Anthropology*. Oxford, UK: Wiley-Blackwell.

Cefkin, M. 2009. *Ethnography and the Corporate Encounter: Reflections on Research In and Of Corporations*. Studies in Public and Applied Anthropology, vol. 5. New York: Berghahn Books.

Chin, Elizabeth. 1999. Ethnically Correct Dolls: Toying with the Race Industry. *American Anthropologist* 101(2): 30–321.

Cherrington, D. J. 1989. *Organizational Behavior*. Boston: Allyn & Bacon.

Classen, Constance, and David Howes. 1996. Epilogue: The Dynamics and Ethics of Cross-Cultural Consumption. In *Cross-Cultural Consumption: Global Markets, Local Realities*, D. Howes (ed.), pp. 178–194. London: Routledge.

Clifford, James. 1988. *The Predicament of Culture: Twentieth Century Ethnography and Art*. Cambridge, MA: Harvard University Press.

Cohen, Colleen Ballerino, Richard Wilk, and Beverly Stoeltje, eds. 1996. *Beauty Queens on the Global Stage*. New York: Routledge.

Connors, Jeanne L., and Thomas A. Romberg. 1991. Middle Management and Quality Control: Strategies for Obstructionism. *Human Organization* 50: 61–65.

Consumer Culture Theory. 2011. About CCT. www.consumerculturetheory.org. (accessed 7/20/2011).

Copeland, M. V. 2010. Intel's Cultural Anthropologist. http://money.cnn.com/2010/09/20/ technology/intel_anthropologists.fortune/index.htm (accessed 9/21/2010).

Costa, Janeen A., and G. Bamossy, eds. 1995. *Marketing in a Multi-Cultural World*. Thousand Oaks, CA: Sage.

Crane, Julia C., and Michael V. Angrosino. 1992. *Field Prospects in Anthropology: A Stu- dents' Handbook*. Long Grove, IL: Waveland Press.

Creighton, Millie R. 1997. Consuming Rural Japan: The Marketing of Tradition and Nostalgia in the Japanese Travel Industry. *Ethnology* 26(3): 239–254.

Creighton, Millie R. 1993. "Sweet Love" and Women's Place: Valentine's Day, Japan Style. *Journal of Popular Culture* 27(3): 1–20.

Creighton, Millie R. 1994. "Edutaining" Children: Consumer and Gender Socialization in Japanese Marketing. *Ethnology* 33(1): 35–52.

Croissant, Jennifer L. 1999. A View from the Basement: The Ethics and Politics of Teach- ing Engineers while Studying Them. *Anthropology of Work Review* 20(1): 22–27.

Dalton, M. 1948. The Industrial Rate-Buster: A Characterization. *Applied Anthropology* 7(1): 1–16.

Darrouzet, Christopher, Helga Wild, and Susann Wilkinson. 2009. Participatory Ethnog- raphy at Work: Practicing in the Puzzle Palaces of a Large, Complex Healthcare Organization. In *Ethnography and the Corporate Encounter: Reflections on Research In and Of Corporations*, M. Cefkin (ed.), pp. 61–94. New York: Berghahn Books.

Deal, Terrence E., and Allan A. Kennedy. 1982. *Corporate Cultures*. Reading, MA: Addi- son-Wesley.

Denny, Rita M. 1995. Speaking to Customers: The Anthropology of Communications. In *Contemporary Marketing and Consumer Behavior*, J. J. Sherry (ed.), pp. 330–345. Thousand Oaks, CA: Sage.

Denny, Rita M. 2002. Communicating with Clients. In *Creating Breakthrough Ideas: The Collaboration of Anthropologists and Designers in the Product Development Industry*, S. Squires and B. Byrne (eds.), pp. 147–159. Westport, CT: Bergin and Garvey.

Dubinskas, Frank A., ed. 1988. *Making Time: Ethnographies of High-Technology Organizations*. Philadelphia: Temple University Press.

Duhaime, Carole, Annamma Joy, and Christopher Ross. 1995. Learning to "See": A Folk Phenomenology of the Consumption of Contemporary Canadian Art. In *Contemporary Marketing and Consumer Behavior: An Anthropological Sourcebook*, J. Sherry (ed.), pp. 351–398. Thousand Oaks, CA: Sage.

Durrenburger, Paul, and Suzan Erem. 2013. American Labor Unions as Organizations. In *A Companion to Organizational Anthropology* Douglas Caulkins and Ann T. Jordan (eds.). Oxford, UK: Wiley-Blackwell.

Edelman, Marc, and Angelique Haugerud, eds. 2005. *The Anthropology of Development and Globalization: From classical political economy to contemporary neoliberalism*. Malden, MA: Blackwell.

Edwards, Walter. 1987. The Commercialized Wedding as Ritual. *Journal of Japanese Studies*. 13(1): 51–78.

EPIC. 2011. The Ethnographic Praxis in Industry Conference. http//www.epiconference.com/ (accessed 7/15/2011).

Fass, Allison. 2001. Advertising. *New York Times*, 14 June, p. C11.

Fernandez, John P. 1991. *Managing a Diverse Work Force*. Lexington, MA: Lexington Books.

Ferraro, Gary P. 2002. *The Cultural Dimension of International Business*. Upper Saddle River, NJ: Prentice-Hall.

Fine, Michelle. 1994. Working the Hyphens: Reinventing Self and Other in Qualitative. Research. In *Handbook of Qualitative Research*, N. Denzin and Yvonna S. Lincoln (eds.), pp. 70–82. Thousand Oaks, CA: Sage.

Fiske, Shirley. 2008. Community Engagement and Cultural Heritage in Fort Apache. *Anthropology News* (May): 41.

Fitzgerald, M. 2006. Intel's Hiring Spree. *Technology Review*, 14 February. Cambridge MA: Massachusetts Institute of Technology. http://www.technologyreview.com/news/405306/intels-hiring-spree/ (accessed 7/17/2012).

Floch, Jean-Marie. 2000. *Visual Identities*. London: Continuum Press.

Fluehr-Lobban, Carolyn, ed. 1991. *Ethics and the Profession of Anthropology*. Philadelphia: University of Pennsylvania Press.

Food Inc. 2009, January 30. Coke Dropping "Classic" Tagline from Logo, NBCNEWS.com. http://www.msnbc.msn.com/id/28932986/ns/business-us_business/t/coke-dropping-classic-tagline-logo/ (accessed 7/20/2012).

Forsythe, Diana E. 1999. Ethics and Politics of Studying Up in Technoscience. *Anthropology of Work Review* 20(1): 6–11.

Franke, Richard H., and James D. Kaul. 1978. The Hawthorne Experiment: First Statistical Interpretation. *American Sociological Review* 43: 623–643.

Gamst, Frederick C. 1977. An Integrating View of the Underlying Premises of an Industrial Ethnology in the United States and Canada. Golden Anniversary Special Issue on Industrial Ethnology. *Anthropological Quarterly* 50: 1–8.

Gamst, Frederick, and Edward Norbeck. 1976. *Ideas of Culture: Sources and Uses*. New York: Holt, Rinehart and Winston.

Garbarino, Merwyn S. 1983 [1977]. *Sociocultural Theory in Anthropology: A Short History*. Long Grove, IL: Waveland Press.

Gardner, Burleigh. 1949. *Human Relations in Industry*. Chicago: R. D. Irwin.

Gardner, Burleigh. 1978. Doing Business with Management. In *Applied Anthropology in America*, E. M. Eddy and W. L. Partridge (eds.), pp. 245–260. New York: Columbia University Press.

Gardner, Burleigh, and William F. Whyte. 1945. The Main in the Middle: Position and Problems of the Foreman. *Applied Anthropology* 6(2).

Gladwin, Thomas. 1964. Culture and Logical Process. In *Explorations in Cultural Anthropology: Essays Presented to George Peter Murdock,* W. Goodenough (ed.). New York: McGraw-Hill.

Gluesing, Julia. 2013. A Mixed-Methods Approach to Understanding Global Networked Organizations. In *A Companion to Organizational Anthropology,* Douglas Caulkins and Ann T. Jordan (eds). Oxford, UK: Wiley-Blackwell.

Graves, William, and Mark Shields. 1991. Rethinking Moral Responsibility in Fieldwork: The Situated Negotiation of Research Ethics in Anthropology and Sociology. In *Ethics and the Profession of Anthropology,* C. Fluehr-Lobban (ed.), Philadelphia: University of Pennsylvania Press.

Grey, Mark A. 1999. Immigrants, Migration, and Worker Turnover at the Hog Pride Pork Packing Plant. *Human Organization* 58(1): 16–27.

Hall, Edward T. 1981. *The Silent Language.* New York: Doubleday.

Hamada, Tomoko. 1988. Working with Japanese: U.S.–Japanese Joint Venture Contract. *Practicing Anthropology* 10(1): 6–7.

Hamada, Tomoko. 1991. *American Enterprise in Japan.* Albany: State University of New York Press.

Hamada, Tomoko. 1995. Inventing Cultural Others in Organizations: A Case of Anthropological Reflexivity in a Multinational Firm. *Journal of Applied Behavioral Science* 31(2): 162–185.

Hamada, Tomoko, and Ann T. Jordan, eds. 1990. Cross-Cultural Management and Organizational Culture. *Studies in Third World Societies,* 42. Williamsburg: College of William and Mary, Department of Anthropology.

Hamann, Edmund T., Saloshna Vandeyar, and Juan Sanchez Garcia. 2013. Organization of Schooling in Three Countries. In *A Companion to Organizational Anthropology,* Douglas Caulkins and Ann T. Jordan (eds.). Oxford, UK: Wiley-Blackwell.

Harris, Marvin. 1968. *The Rise of Anthropological Theory: A History of Theories of Culture.* New York: Crowell.

Harris, Philip R., and Robert T. Moran. 1987. *Managing Cultural Difference,* Second Edition. Houston: Gulf Publishing.

Hiebert, Paul G. 1976. *Cultural Anthropology.* Philadelphia: J. B. Lippincott.

Ho, Karen. 2009. Disciplining Investment Bankers, Disciplining the Economy: Wall Street's Institutional Culture of Crisis and the Downsizing of "Corporate America." *American Anthropologist* 111(2): 177–189.

Hofstead, Geert. 1980. *Culture's Consequences: International Differences in Work-Related Values.* Beverly Hills: Sage.

Holcombe, Sarah E., and Patrick Sullivan. 2013. Australian Indigenous Organizations. In *A Companion to Organizational Anthropology,* Douglas Caulkins and Ann T. Jordan (eds.). Oxford, UK: Wiley-Blackwell.

Howes, David. 1996a. Introduction: Commodities and Cultural Borders. In *Cross-Cultural Consumption: Global Markets, Local Realities,* D. Howes (ed.), pp. 1–18. London: Routledge.

Howes, David, ed. 1996b. *Cross-Cultural Consumption: Global Markets, Local Realities.* London: Routledge.

Hume, S. 1990. How Big Mac Made It to Moscow. *Advertising Age,* 22 January, 61(4): 16.

Jones, Del. 1999. Hot Asset in Corporate: Anthropology Degrees. *USA Today,* 18 February, 1B.

Jordan, Ann T. 1989. Organizational Culture: It's Here, But Is It Anthropology? *Anthropology of Work Review* 10(3): 2–5.

Jordan, Ann T. 1990. Organizational Culture and Culture Change: A Case Study. In *Cross-Cultural Management and Organizational Culture,* T. Hamada and A. T. Jordan (eds.), *Studies in Third World Societies,* p. 42. Williamsburg: College of William and Mary, Department of Anthropology.

Jordan, Ann T. 1999. An Anthropological Approach to the Study of Organizational Change: The Move to Self-Managed Work Teams. *Practicing Anthropology* 21(4): 14–19.

Jordan, Ann T. 2011. *The Making of a Modern Kingdom: Globalization and Change in Saudi Arabia*. Long Grove, IL: Waveland Press.

Jordan, Ann T., Elizabeth Briody, et al. 2009. Consumer Car Purchasing Behavior. University of North Texas, Department of Anthropology. Class Project in Organizational Anthropology. Unpublished Manuscript.

Jordan, Ann T. and Douglas Caulkins. 2013. Expanding the Field of Organizational Anthropology for the Twenty-first Century. In *A Companion to Organizational Anthropology*, Douglas Caulkins and Ann T. Jordan (eds.). Oxford, UK: Wiley-Blackwell.

Jordan, Brigitte, and Austin Henderson. 1995. Interaction Analysis: Foundations and Practice. *Journal of the Learning Sciences* 4(1): 39–103.

Joy, Annamma, Michael Hui, Chankon Kim, and Michel Laroche. 1995. The Cultural Past in the Present: The Meaning of Home and Objects in the Homes of Working-Class Italian Immigrants in Montreal. In *Marketing in a Multicultural World: Ethnicity, Nationalism, and Cultural Identity*, J. A. Costa and G. J. Bamossy (eds.), pp. 145–179. Thousand Oaks CA: Sage.

Kaprow, Miriam Lee. 1991. Magical Work: Firefighters in New York. *Human Organization* 50(1): 97–103.

Kaprow, Miriam Lee. 1999. The Last, Best Work: Firefighters in the Fire Department of New York. *Anthropology of Work Review* 19(2): 5–25.

Kates, Steven M., and Russell W. Belk. 2001. The Meanings of Lesbian and Gay Pride Day: Resistance through Consumption and Resistance to Consumption. *Journal of Contemporary Ethnography* 30(4): 392–429.

Keesing, Roger M., and Felix M. Keesing. 1971. *New Perspectives in Cultural Anthropology*. New York: Holt, Rinehart and Winston.

Kogod, K. 1994. The Bridges Process: Enhancing Organizational Cultures to Support Diversity. In *Practicing Anthropology in Corporate America: Consulting on Organizational Culture*, Ann T. Jordan, ed. National Association for the Practice of Anthropology Bulletin 14. Washington, DC: American Anthropological Association.

Krause Jensen, Jakob. 2010 *Flexible Firm: The Design of Culture at Bang& Olufsen*. Oxford: Berghahn Books.

Kramer, Andrew E. 2010. Russia's Evolution, Seen through Golden Arches. *New York Times*, 1 February. www.nytimes.com/2010/02/02/business/global/02mcdonalds.html?_r=1 (accessed 4/12/2012).

Kroeber, Alfred, and Clyde Kluckhohn. 1952. *Culture: A Critical Review of Concepts and Definitions* (Papers of the Peabody Museum of American Archaeology and Ethnology, Vol. 47). Cambridge, MA: Harvard University Press.

Lessinger, Johanna. 1992. Nonresident Indian Investment and India's Drive for Industrial Modernization. In *Anthropology and the Global Factory: Studies of the New Industrialization in the Late Twentieth Century*, F. A. Rothstein and M. L. Blim (eds.), pp. 62–82. New York: Bergin and Garvey.

Litzinger, Ralph. 2006. Contested Sovereignties and the Critical Ecosystem Partnership Fund. *PoLAR: Political and Legal Anthropology Review* 29(1): 66-87.

Malefyt, Timothy deWaal. 2009. How Consumers Create Value in a Recession Economy. *EPIC 2009*, pp. 209–220. American Anthropological Association.

Malefyt, Timothy deWaal, and Brian Moeran. 2003. *Advertising Cultures*. Oxford: Berg.

Malefyt, Timothy deWaal, and Robert J. Morais. 2012. *Advertising and Anthropology: Ethnographic Practice and Cultural Perspectives*. London: Berg.

Malinowski, Bronislaw. 1984 [1922]. *Argonauts of the Western Pacific*. Long Grove, IL: Waveland Press.

Marcus, George E., ed. 1998. *Corporate Futures: The Diffusion of the Culturally Sensitive Corporate Form*. Chicago: University of Chicago Press.

Marcus, George E., and Michael J. M. Fischer. 1968. *Anthropology as Cultural Critique: An Experimental Moment in the Human Sciences*. Chicago: University of Chicago Press.

McCracken, Grant. 1988. *Culture and Consumption*. Bloomington: Indiana University Press.

McCracken, Grant. 1995. *Big Hair: A Journey into the Transformation of Self.* Woodstock, NY: The Overlook Press.

McCurdy, David W., James P. Spradley, and Dianna J. Shandy. 2005. *The Cultural Experience: Ethnography in Complex Society,* 2nd ed. Long Grove, IL: Waveland Press.

McDonald's. 2012. McDonald's Worldwide http://www.mcdonalds.ca/ca/en/our_story/mcdonalds_worldwide.html (accessed 4/10/2012).

Miller, Daniel. 1997. *Capitalism: An Ethnographic Approach.* Oxford: Berg.

Miller, Daniel, ed. 1998. *Material Cultures: Why Some Things Matter.* Chicago: University of Chicago Press.

Morey, Nancy C., and Fred Luthans. 1984. An Emic Perspective and Ethnoscience Methods for Organizational Research. *Academy of Management Review* 9: 27–36.

Moeran, Brian, and Christina Garsten. 2011. What's in a Name? Editors' Introduction to the Journal of Business Anthropology. *Journal of Business Anthropology* 1(1):1–19.

Morrill, Calvin. 1991. The Customs of Conflict Management among Corporate Executives. *American Anthropologist* 93(4): 871–893.

Mulhare, Eileen. 1999. Mindful of the Future: Strategic Planning Ideology and the Culture of Nonprofit Management. *Human Organization* 58(3): 323–330.

Nardi, Bonnie A. 2007. Placeless Organizations: Collaborating for Transformation. *Mind, Culture, and Activity.* 14(1-2): 5–22.

Neyland, Daniel. 2013. The Ethnography of Numbers. In *A Companion to Organizational Anthropology,* Douglas Caulkins and Ann T. Jordan (eds.). Oxford, UK: Wiley-Blackwell.

Novo, Carmen Martinez. 2013. Why Are Indigenous Organizations Declining in Latin America? In *A Companion to Organizational Anthropology,* Douglas Caulkins and Ann T. Jordan (eds.). Oxford, UK: Wiley-Blackwell.

Ofem, Brandon, Theresa M. Floyd, and Stephen P. Borgatti. 2013. Social Networks and Organizations. In *A Companion to Organizational Anthropology,* Douglas Caulkins and Ann T. Jordan (eds). Oxford, UK: Wiley Blackwell Publishing.

Ojile, Constance S. 1986. Intercultural Training: An Overview of the Benefits for Business and the Anthropologist's Emerging Role. In *Anthropology and International Business,* H. Serrie (ed.), pp. 35–51. Studies in Third World Societies, 28. Williamsburg: College of William and Mary, Department of Anthropology.

Oldani, Michael J. 1999. Profit Makers vs. Profit Takers. *Anthropology News* (November): 7–8.

Olsen, Barbara 1995. Brand Loyalty and Consumption Patterns: The Lineage Factor. In *Contemporary Marketing and Consumer Behavior: An Anthropological Sourcebook,* J. Sherry (ed.), pp. 245–281. Thousand Oaks, CA: Sage.

Orr, Julian E. 1990. Sharing Knowledge, Celebrating Identity: Community Memory in a Service Culture. In *Collective Remembering,* D. Middleton and D. Edwards (eds.), pp. 169–189. London: Sage.

Ortlieb, Martin. 2011. Unclear Social Etiquette Online: How Users Experiment (And Struggle) with Interacting across Many Channels and Devices in an Ever-Evolving and Fast-Changing Landscape of Communication Tools. *EPIC 2011,* pp. 311–321. American Anthropological Association.

Ouchi, William. 1981. *Theory Z.* Reading, MA: Addison-Wesley.

Pascale, Richard Tanner, and Anthony G. Athos. 1981. *The Art of Japanese Management.* New York: Simon and Schuster.

Peacock, James. 1997. The Future of Anthropology. *American Anthropologist* 99(1): 9–29.

Peinado, Alice, Magdalena Jarvin, and Juliette Damoisel. 2011. What Happens When You Mix Bankers, Insurers, Consultants, Anthropologists and Designers: The Saga of Project FiDJI in France. *EPIC 2011,* pp. 256–276. American Anthropological Association.

Peters, Thomas J., and Robert H. Waterman. 1982. *In Search of Excellence.* New York: Warner Books.

Philibert, Jean-Marc, and Christine Jourdan. 1996. Perishable Goods: Modes of Consumption in the Pacific Islands. In *Cross-Cultural Consumption: Global Markets, Local Realities*, D. Howes (ed.), pp. 55–76. London: Routledge.

Press, Irwin. 1997. The Quality Movement in U.S. Health Care: Implications for Anthropology. *Human Organization* 56(1): 1–8.

Price, Linda L., and Eric J. Arnould. 1999. Commercial Friendships: Service Provider-Client Relationships in Context. *Journal of Marketing* 63(October): 38–56.

Rand, Erica. 1995. *Barbie's Queer Accessories*. Durham, NC: Duke University Press.

Regional Language Network London. 2008. Managing a Multicultural Workforce: Languages and Culture at Work in Your Business. RLN Business Guides. www.rln-london.com/multicultural (accessed 2/14/2012).

Richardson, F. L. W., and C. R. Walker. 1948. *Human Relations in an Expanding Company: A Study of the Manufacturing Departments in the Endicott Plant of the International Business Machines Corporation*. New Haven, CT: Yale University, Labor Management Center.

Rodrigue, Jean-Paul, Claude Corntois, and Brian Slack. 2009. *The Geography of Transport Systems*, 2nd ed. New York: Routledge.

Roseberry, William, Lowell Gudmundson, and K. Mario Samper, eds. 1995. *Coffee, Society and Power in Latin America*. Baltimore: Johns Hopkins University Press.

Røyrvik, Emil. 2011. *The Allure of Capitalism: An Ethnography of Management and the Global Economy in Crisis*. Oxford: Berghahn Books.

Sacher, Heiko K. 2002. Semiotics as Common Ground: Connecting the Cultures of Analysis and Creation. In *Creating Breakthrough Ideas: The Collaboration of Anthropologists and Designers in the Product Development Industry*, S. Squires and B. Byrne (eds.), pp. 175–195. Westport, CT: Bergin and Garvey.

Sachs, Patricia, ed. 1989. Anthropological Approaches to Organizational Culture. Theme Issue. *Anthropology of Work Review* 10(3).

Salzman, Philip Carl. 2001. *Understanding Culture: An Introduction to Anthropological Theory*. Long Grove, IL: Waveland Press.

Sanday, Peggy Reeves. 1979. The Ethnographic Paradigm(s). *Administrative Science Quarterly* 24: 527–538.

Sayles, L. R. 1952. A Case Study of Urban Participation and Technological Change. *Human Organization* 11(1): 5–15.

Schneider, Mary Jo. 1998. The Wal-Mart Annual Meeting: From Small-Town America to a Global Corporate Culture. *Human Organization* 57(3): 292–299.

Schwartzman, Helen B. 1989. *The Meeting: Gatherings in Organizations and Communities*. New York: Plenum Press.

Schwartzman, Helen B. 1993. *Ethnography in Organizations*. Newbury Park, CA: Sage.

Serrie, Hendrick, ed. 1986. *Anthropology and International Business*. Studies in Third World Societies, 28. Williamsburg: College of William and Mary, Department of Anthropology.

Serrie, Hendrick. 1999. Training Chinese Managers for Leadership: Six Cross-Cultural Principles. *Practicing Anthropology* 21(4): 35–41.

Shaffer, Scarlet. 2008. Further Resources for Careers in Applied Anthropology. *NAPA Bulletin* 29, pp 195–205. American Anthropological Association.

Sherry, John. 1999. Ethnography and Internet Time: Ethics, Politics and Practice. *Anthropology of Work Review* 20(1): 15–21.

Sherry, John F., ed. 1995. *Contemporary Marketing and Consumer Behavior: An Anthropological Sourcebook*. Thousand Oaks, CA: Sage.

Sherry, John F., ed. 1998. *ServiceScapes: The Concept of Place in Contemporary Markets*. Chicago: NTC Business Books.

Sherry, John F., Robert V. Kozinets, Diana Storm, Adam Duhachek, Krittinee Nuttavuthisit, and Benet DeBerry-Spence. 2001. Being in the Zone: Staging Retail Theater at ESPN Zone Chicago. *Journal of Contemporary Ethnography* 30(4): 465–510.

Sibley, Willis E., and Tomoko Hamada, eds. 1994. *Anthropological Perspectives on Organizational Culture*. Washington, DC: University Press of America.

Sobo, E. J., C. Bowman, G. A. Aarons, et al. 2008. Enhancing Organizational Change and Improvement Prospects: Lessons from an HIV Testing Intervention for Veterans. *Human Organization*, 67(4): 443–454.

Spradley, James P. 1980. *Participant Observation*. New York: Holt, Rinehart and Winston.

Squires, Susan. 2002. Doing the Work: Customer Research in the Product Development and Design Industry. In *Creating Breakthrough Ideas: The Collaboration of Anthropologists and Designers in the Product Development Industry*, S. Squires and B. Byrne (eds.), pp. 103–124. Westport, CT: Bergin and Garvey.

Stern, Barbara B., Craig J. Thompson, and Eric J. Arnould. 1998. Narrative Analysis of a Marketing Relationship: The Consumer's Perspective. *Communication Abstracts* 21(6): 195–213.

Suchman, Lucy. 1987. *Plans and Situated Actions: The Problem of Human–Machine Communication*. New York: Cambridge University Press.

Sunderland, Patricia L., and Rita M. Denny. 2007. *Doing Anthropology in Consumer Research*. Walnut Creek, CA: Left Coast Press.

SUSPS. 2012. Population Numbers, Projections, Graphs, and Data. http://www.susps.org/overview/numbers.html (accessed 6/28/2012).

Tani, Masakuzu, and William L. Rathje. 1995. Consumer Behavior Reflected in Discards: A Case Study of Dry-Cell Batteries. In *Contemporary Marketing and Consumer Behavior: An Anthropological Sourcebook*, J. Sherry (ed.), pp. 86–104. Thousand Oaks, CA: Sage.

Terpstra, Vern, and Kenneth David. 1985. *The Cultural Environment of International Business*. Cincinnati: Southwestern Publishing.

Tobin, Joseph J. 1992. Introduction: Domesticating the West. In *Re-made in Japan: Everyday Life and Consumer Taste in a Changing Society*, J. J. Tobin (ed.), pp. 1–41. New Haven, CT: Yale University Press.

Trice, Hanson, and Janice Beyer. 1993. *The Cultures of Work Organizations*. Englewood Cliffs, NJ: Prentice-Hall.

Trotter, Robert T., Gulcin H. Sengir, and Elizabeth K. Briody. 2008. The Cultural Processes of Partnerships. In *Partnering for Organizational Performance*, E. K. Briody and R. T. Trotter (eds.). Lanham, MD: Rowman and Littlefield.

US Census Bureau: State and County QuickFacts. 2012. http://quickfacts.census.gov/qfd/states/00000.html (accessed 7/18/2012).

Van Marrewijk, Alfons. 2010. European Developments in Business Anthropology. *International Journal of Business Anthropology* 1(1).

Van Veggel, Rob. n.d. Where Two Sides of Ethnography Collide. Unpublished manuscript.

Villaveces-Izquierdo, Santiago. 1998. Colombo-Japanese Mixtures amidst a Corporate Reinvention. In *Corporate Futures: The Diffusion of the Culturally Sensitive Corporate Form*, G. Marcus (ed.), pp. 113–140. Chicago: University of Chicago Press.

Walck, Christa L., and Ann T. Jordan. 1993. Using Ethnographic Techniques in the Organizational Behavior Classroom. *Journal of Management Education* 17(2): 197–217.

Walker, Charles R., and Robert H. Guest. 1952. *The Man on the Assembly Line*. Cambridge, MA: Harvard University Press.

Wasson, Christina. 2000. Ethnography in the Field of Design. *Human Organization* 59(4): 377–388.

Wasson, Christina. 2002. Collaborative Work: Integrating the Roles of Ethnographers and Designers. In *Creating Breakthrough Ideas: Using Ethnographic Research in the Product Development Industry*, S. Squires and B. Byrne (eds.), pp. 71–90. Westport CT: Greenwood Publishing Group.

Wasson, Christina. 2013. Virtual Organizations. In *A Companion to Organizational Anthropology*, Douglas Caulkins and Ann T. Jordan (eds.). Oxford, UK: Wiley-Blackwell.

Weise, Elizabeth. 1999. Companies Learn Value of Grass Root Anthropologist Help Adapt Products to World's Cultures. In *USA Today*. 26 May, p. 4d.

Whyte, William Foote. 1948. Incentives for Productivity: The Case of the Bundy Tubing Company. *Applied Anthropology* 7(2): 1–16.

Whyte, William Foote. 1951. *Pattern for Industrial Peace*. New York: Harper and Row.

Whyte, William Foote. 1961. *Men at Work*. Homewood, IL: Dorsey Press.

Wilk, Richard R. 1991. *Household Ecology: Economic Change and Domestic Life among the Kekchi Maya in Belize*. Tucson: University of Arizona.

Wilson, Thomas M. 1995. Blurred Borders: Local and Global Consumer Culture in Northern Ireland. In *Marketing in a Multicultural World*, J. A. Costa and G. J. Bamossy (eds.), pp. 231–256. Thousand Oaks, CA: Sage.

Index